Womanrunes
Interpretation Guide

Molly Remer
and Shekhinah Mountainwater

2014, first edition
2018, second edition
Brigid's Grove
www.brigidsgrove.com

Womanrunes
Interpretation Guide

© *Interpretations, rune-specific layouts, and text copyright 2014, 2018*
Molly Remer, MSW, M.Div, D.Min

© *System and symbols copyright 1988*
Shekhinah Mountainwater

First Edition 2014
Second Edition 2018

ISBN-13:
978-1725083264

ISBN-10:
1725083264

Cover design, tree goddess logo, layout, and illustrations by Mark Remer

Produced in cooperation with the estate of Shekhinah Mountainwater (ShekhinahWorks).

In memory of Shekhinah Mountainwater. You inspired me and I am honored to carry on your work.

Brigid's Grove
www.brigidsgrove.com

Listen to what is walking here
tiptoeing through your dreams
knocking at the door of your unconscious mind
whispering from shadows
calling from the full moon
twinkling in the stars
carried by the night wind woman
rising at sunset
peeking out
in tentative
yet persistent purpose.
Listen to the call
trust the talkative silence...

Contents

Introduction 7

About Shekhinah Mountainwater 11

About Womanrunes 13

The Runes 19

Interpretations 23

Rune Layouts 139

Engaging with the Runes 183

Original Womanrunes Handouts 200

About the Author 203

Acknowledgments 204

Resources 206

Introduction

Womanrunes are a unique and powerful divination system that use simple, woman-identified symbols to connect deeply with your own inner wisdom as well as the flow of womanspirit knowledge that surrounds you. Used as a personal oracle, they offer spiritual insight, understanding, and guidance as well as calls to action and discovery. People who use them are amazed to discover how the symbols and interpretations reach out with exactly what is needed in that moment. Women's experiences with Womanrunes are powerful, magical, inspirational, potent, and mystical. The wisdom within them can be drawn upon again and again, often uncovering new information, understanding, and truth with each reading.

The simplest and most common use for Womanrunes is to draw a rune daily or when you feel an intuitive need for guidance. Draw the rune and *feel* into it. What is it sharing with you? Read the companion interpretation and let it soak in. These symbols speak to something deep within you. You may have the experience of feeling *heard* and *answered* when you choose a rune and read its interpretation.

Womanrunes provide a pathway to your own "truth-sense." They open you up to your own internal guidance and to messages and inspiration from the Goddess, the Earth, or your spiritual guides.

Womanrunes may also be used to do guidance readings for friends or clients. Messages from Womanrunes are not prescriptive or directive, instead they serve as a rich conduit to exactly what you need to hear and receive in that moment.

We are surrounded every day by divine inspiration, information, and guidance. It may appear in mundane, ordinary ways or in surprising and mystical ways. The natural world also provides us with many sacred messages (whether we perceive these messages as from the Goddess, our guides, Spirit, or simply the creative energies of time and place). This wisdom may often be soft and subtle. Using oracle tools helps us become more attuned and receptive to these experiences and as we become more receptive we encourage even more of them to occur. Womanrunes invite the inspiration and guidance in, offering animated, intimate, living, interactive experiences with divinity. A conduit is formed between you, the soul, and the divine when you use these symbols.

Many people also find it satisfying to draw or carve Womanrunes onto art, calendars, sculptures and more. Used in this way, Womanrunes can attract their messages deeply into your life or can serve as potent declarations of intention.

Why Such Simple Images?

Many divination and oracle systems include beautiful artwork on the cards. Womanrunes are simple symbols and are, in fact, a type of symbol writing that speaks to a deep part of the soul. The clean focus and simplicity of the Womanrunes symbols evoke rich messages and soul guidance in their own special way that differs from the image-rich paintings of other systems. They are also very easy to use directly yourself—including them in your own art, drawing or etching them onto objects, and thereby writing them into your consciousness in a *living* manner. Used as a dynamic, hands-on, participatory system, Womanrunes become part of your own language of the Divine, the Goddess, your inner wisdom, and womanspirit truths.

In Dianne Skafte's book *Listening to the Oracle*, she writes: "Symbols should be used as springboards into oracular space, where the real story will be found...by opening a wide space for the realities that pay us a visit in dreams, oracles, and other mysterious domains, we will be met by many guides to the soul" (p. 54).

About Shekhinah Mountainwater

Make for yourself a power spot
Bring you a spoon and a cooking pot
Bring air
Bring fire
Bring water
Bring earth
And a new universe you will birth...
–Shekhinah Mountainwater in The Goddess Celebrates by Diane Stein

I was interested in Goddess spirituality for many years before eventually discovering Shekhinah Mountainwater. When I did, she'd already passed away. I bought a used copy of her book *Ariadne's Thread* and fell in love with it. I learned about her Womanrunes and fell in love with them even more. In the book I quote above, Shehkinah describes herself in this way:

"...I have taken vows to be a full-time priestess and Goddess-worker. I teach classes, make ceremony, develop calendars and culture, write, play music, create art and poetry. I long for a society where women and men are free to be themselves, to be creative and loving and fulfilled in all their great potential..." (p. 86)

Shekhinah was a foremother of Goddess spirituality and discovered the Goddess in the early 1970's. She began teaching, writing, and singing with an emphasis on women's spirituality and worked as a priestess with women's circles from the 1970's until her death in 2007.

In Shekhinah's own words in her classic book *Ariadne's Thread:*

> "I am a lover, a mother, a daughter, and a sister of women. I am a priestess, a teacher, a writer, an artist, a scholar, a musician, tarot and runemaker, reader of tarot and runes, a craftswoman, a ritualist, a healer, and a changer. I am a wild and watery woman, a magical mystical poet...a weaver of song and myth. I am a founding mother of the women's spirituality movement, one of the first to channel Goddess revolution in our times" (p. 380).

About Womanrunes

*May I be open to magic in all of its
wild, mysterious, surprising, and beautiful forms.
May my heart be light
and may my shoulders soften easily.
May I have no fear of my own power
and may I walk through my other fears with courage.
May I live, laugh, and love with awareness
And may I experience this day
wisely, wonderfully, and well.*

Runes are a type of magical writing or magical alphabet system used for divination, communication, and understanding of self and cosmos. The most commonly seen runes today derive from old Celtic runes of Europe. Some mythic evidence indicates that these were first invented and used by women, possibly gifted to them by the Norns, the three Goddesses of Fate. They are also associated with the God Odin.

The Birth of Womanrunes

Womanrunes are a system of forty-one female-identified symbols for divination, self-development, and personal growth. They were created by Shekhinah Mountainwater in 1987 and introduced in her book *Ariadne's Thread* in 1991.

In 1987 after having worked with traditional runes, but sensing "something more" behind them, Shekhinah's friend suggested she create a specifically woman-identified rune system. On the Summer Solstice of that year, Shekhinah explains, "goddess-lightning struck. I fell into a state of enchantment and, in a single day, the symbols for my Womanrunes were born… Suddenly I was liberated, and the new symbols poured out beneath my pen. Like the priestesses of old, I opened myself, and the Goddess sent me Her magic" (p. 219).

In 2012, I was reading a back issue of SageWoman magazine from 1988 and stumbled across an article about Womanrunes. I instantly fell in love with them. They issued a powerful call to me. I scoured the internet for more information, where I eventually found a handout and pronunciation guide (reprinted on page 201). I purchased Shekhinah's book, *Ariadne's Thread*, and began making Womanrunes sets at women's spirituality retreats with my friends.

As a priestess and ritual facilitator, I shared the basic list of Womanrunes with my women's circle and we adopted them as a special part of our group, using them on a variety of group projects. Shekhinah's book, *Ariadne's Thread*, explains that Womanrunes are very intuitive and can readily be interpreted using your own inherent sense of their meanings.

However, I also observed that many women wished for additional explanations of each rune beyond Shekhinah's original titles and brief keywords.

The depth of my connection to the symbols led me to begin to develop more extensive interpretations of the meaning of each rune. I began a personal practice of drawing one rune and then going to a sacred place in the woods with it to see what it had to tell me. Using this process I created a developed interpretation of the meaning of each rune.

Accessing Our Truth-Sense

In the book *Runes of the Goddess,* author PMH Atwater uses a set of 16 runes based on the ancient Elder Futhark runes and she calls them Goddess runes. With regard to the significance and meaning of runes as a divination systems, she explains:

"Runic symbols are not magic in and of themselves. Symbols are illustrative, not directive. The magic comes from the way they stimulate feelings, emotions, and memories in the one who uses them. Forgotten wisdoms hidden within the psyche begin to awaken and resurface. This is the real magic… uncovering the deeper depths of your own being." (p. 24)

She goes on to explain:

"Learning the way of a cast utilizes sacred play to help you step into your own 'dream' (the life you live) so you can view issues from another perspective. This enables you to develop an ongoing pathway into the heart and soul of your 'truth-sense,' that intuitive wellspring at the central core of all that you are. Once the pathway is developed, you can almost magically move beyond sacred play into a kind of 'flow' state where 'moment matches mind.' This is synchronicity—where random events cease to be random, and seemingly unrelated things link together in meaningful and wonderful ways." (p. 26)

This is what I experienced in the woods with the Womanrunes: a pathway to my own "truth-sense." Atwater's description of how she first saw and connected with these runes reminds me of my own experience with Womanrunes. They called to me and spoke to me in ways I continue to explore and uncover.

With Shekhinah's Womanrunes, I felt an irresistible intuitive connection at first contact, but I needed something *more* than their original one to three word descriptions. My friends, too, expressed this need. We made runesets together and they said, "now what? How do we actually read and use these? We need more!" In what eventually became a year-long project, I began deepening into the meaning of each rune individually while alone in a sacred place in the woods and writing an interpretation based on this intuitive information.

We first published an interpretation guidebook for Womanrunes in 2014. After four more years of working with the runes every single day and receiving more information from them, this second edition of the book you are now holding was born.

The Runes

0:	○	The Circle	*Rune of the Self.*	*p. 24*
1:	⏶	The Witch's Hat	*Rune of Magic.*	*p. 27*
2:	☾	The Crescent Moon.	*Rune of Divination.*	*p. 29*
3:	▽	The Yoni	*Rune of Making.*	*p. 32*
4:	♌	The Flame	*Rune of Fire.*	*p. 35*
5:	♡	The Heart	*Rune of Love.*	*p. 37*
6:	⚚	The Labrys	*Rune of Will.*	*p. 40*
7:	⚲	The Dancing Woman	*Rune of Power.*	*p. 44*
8:	□	The Box	*Rune of Boundaries.*	*p. 47*
9:	●	The Dark Moon	*Rune of Wisdom.*	*p. 50*
10:	☯	The Wheel	*Rune of Fate.*	*p. 53*
11:	⚲	The Pendulum	*Rune of Patterns.*	*p. 56*
12:	⚯	The Reflection	*Rune of Surrender.*	*p. 59*
13:	⚱	The Flying Woman	*Rune of Transformation.*	*p. 62*
14:	⚱	The Cauldron	*Rune of Alchemy.*	*p. 65*
15:	☾	The Whole Moon	*Rune of Cycles.*	*p. 68*
16:	∫	The Serpent	*Rune of Awakening.*	*p. 71*
17:	⛤	The Moon and Star.	*Rune of Faith.*	*p.74*

18:	The Sun	Rune of Healing.	p. 77
19:	The Dancing Women	Rune of Celebration.	p. 79
20:	The Great Wheel	Rune of Infinity.	p. 82
21:	The Egg	Rune of Naming.	p. 84
22:	The Sisters	Rune of Friendship.	p. 87
23:	The Seed	Rune of Waiting.	p. 90
24:	The Tool	Rune of Labor.	p. 93
25:	The Winged Circle	Rune of Freedom.	p. 96
26:	The Cauldron of Reflection	Rune of Solitude.	p. 98
27:	The Crowned Heart	Rune of Unconditional Love.	p. 101
28:	The Tree	Rune of Prosperity.	p. 103
29:	The Pentacle	Rune of Protection.	p. 106
30:	The Two Circles	Rune of Merging.	p. 109
31:	The Two Triangles	Rune of Focus.	p. 111
32:	Moonboat	Rune of Journeys.	p. 113
33:	The Hearth	Rune of Nurturance.	p. 115
34:	The Cauldron of Dancing Women	Rune of Honor.	p. 119

35:	The Broom	*Rune of Purification.*	p. 122
36:	The Spiral	*Rune of Initiation.*	p. 125
37:	The Wand	*Rune of Blessing.*	p. 128
38:	The Sun and Moon	*Rune of Laughter.*	p. 131
39:	The Winged Heart	*Rune of Ecstasy.*	p. 133
40:	The Veil	*Rune of Mystery.*	p. 136

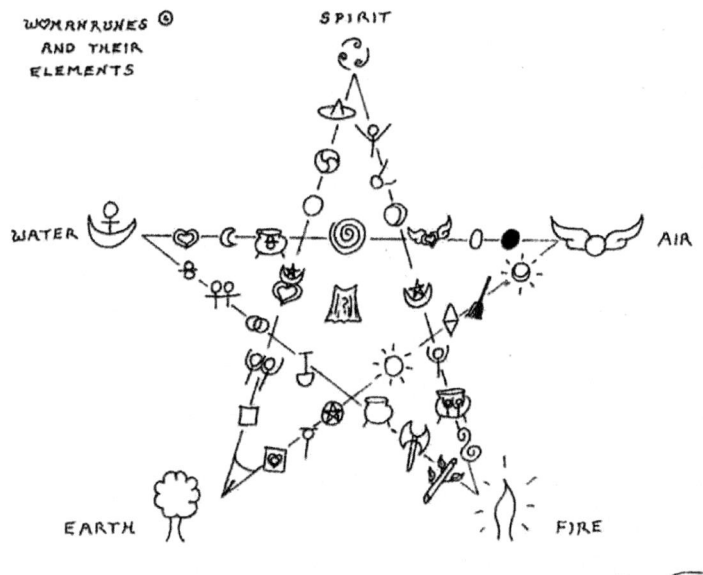

WOMANRUNES AND THEIR ELEMENTS

SPIRIT

WATER — AIR

EARTH   FIRE

©1999 Shekhinah Mountainwater   Please use and acknowledge.   Please keep system intact - Thanks!

Interpretations

o: The Circle

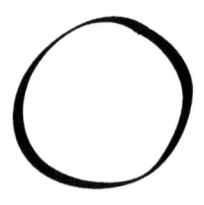

O

Rune of the Self. Beginnings. Potential. Innocence.

The truth of *being* may be grander and deeper and broader than you can ever imagine. Look before you and bear witness to the magic, the pure potentiality that surrounds you all the time. Is not your very Self a true *miracle?* Thinking, breathing, moving, walking, grasping, laughing, loving, writing, talking, holding, birthing, creating. These systems that animate your body, beat your heart, grow your fingernails, circulate your blood, digest your food, gaze at your baby. This is *incredible.* Incredibly majestic, incredibly miraculous, and incredibly mysterious.

What is this process of cell division? What is this process of thought? What is this process of life and living? Where does it come from and where does it go? How does it work? *Really work.* The language of cell division and synapses is not enough. We can explain life in scientific terms...but underlying it is still a fundamental majesty of unimaginable wonder.

Fresh starts. New beginnings. Possibility. Potential. Ripe with promise. The circle is where it all begins, and ends. Maybe there is no beginning and there is no end, but a continuous loop of possibility and promise. Self-contained. Whole. Complete unto itself, needing nothing, just whole.

What is beginning for you?
What do you need for yourself?
Do you feel a sense of potential and promise?
How would you treat yourself if you viewed yourself as innocent?
Do you feel something waiting to start for you?

The Circle rune may indicate that you're at a starting point. That you're ready for something new. That something is beginning or emerging for you. It is a fresh, possible, innocent rune, one that sees with new ideas and fresh perspectives. One that is encompassing and embracing, while also being whole and contained.

How are you tending to yourself? What is beginning for you? What potential feels like it is ready for you to tap into? This rune reminds us to pay attention to the everyday miracles around us, including our own breaths.

Sometimes the Circle shows up when you need to take care of yourself, when being a bit selfish is what is called for, rather than focusing outward on others. It may indicate a need to focus on your own needs, wishes, desires, and plans and to be unconcerned with what others may think of what you are doing or choosing. It may indicate a need to bring your awareness in, to the answers within. It may also indicate the need to approach a situation, problem or experience with the eyes of innocence and the assumption of positive intent and kind potential.

Let it begin with you.

Just as the acorn holds limitless oaks, the Self has limitless potential. Expanding, contracting, opening, closing, leaping, pausing, watching, knowing, asking questions…

Pause and witness the miracle.

1: The Witch's Hat

Rune of Magic. Spells. Enchantment.

This is a rune of naming and claiming and owning and doing. This is a rune of creation, of webweaving, spellcasting, and magicmaking. This is rune of celebration and of *showing up*. What have you been afraid to claim? What name have you been afraid to speak? What scares you to step forward and own?

We all have magic within us, boiling in our cauldron of being. Keeping time with our heartsong, crackling out through our fingertips, waiting to be expressed and sung into being. What enchants you? What needs your sparkle and spice? What needs your magic? What spell are you casting? Is it a conscious one? One with purpose, intention, and focus? Or is it unconscious and still forming?

What is your magic? How do you make magic? Experience magic? Are you enchanted by your life? Where do you feel most magical? How or where or when do you encounter magic? Do you feel connected to your magic?

This rune reminds you that we live in a magical world. Magic is at your fingertips and within you. The Witch's Hat encourages you to claim your magic. To stand up for your magic. To simply BE magic. It reminds you to see the enchantment in daily living and to consciously engage with the world and with your own magic. It may emerge when magical working is needed or simply to remind you of your own magic and power. It often appears as an affirmation and a celebration of the magic you already weave in your world.

Is it time to sweep off the hat and step forward bold and proud? Or is it time to scoop it up and put it on saying, "This is me. This is who I am." You are capable, you are creative, you are alive. You are the enchantress. You are magic. Gather up your resources. Collect your attention. Stir up your power. Step forth with boldness.

This is me. A magical woman. And, yes, that pointed hat is mine.

2: The Crescent Moon

Rune of Divination. Ritual. Door to unconscious.

The Moon Mother calls you. She dances around the edges of your conscious awareness, singing your name, tugging at your spirit. Listen to the Dreamtime...

What is knocking at the doorway of your soul?
What calls to you in the night?
Are you dreaming?
Have you given up on dreams?
Are you listening?
Have you stopped trying?
Do you remember your dreams?
Do you heed their messages?

The Goddess speaks in the language of dreamtime, from deep, dark places and in fuzzy, sleepy awareness. Tune in, look inside, wait for wisdom. It wants to enter, it's on its way. Carried by the moon, drifting in starlight, singing to you, drawing you near. Moon Mother, Dream Mother. Winds of change and destiny are swirling.

Pay attention, take heed, become conscious. In the seemingly coincidental connections and links of life your unconscious, your deep self is speaking to you. She knows many things.

Divination is not about predicting the future, but about understanding your path and heeding the guidance laid out before you in many bright, sparkling, starry, and shadowy ways. She speaks in dreams, speaks in nudges, speaks in signs, signals, synchronicities. This is the language of symbol, myth, pattern, and magic.

There are messages surrounding you. Oracles of the everyday. Doorways to magic.

Do you make time for regular divination? What does divination mean to you?

Make space for personal, daily rituals of connection and understanding. Listen to your dreams. Listen to the whispers of your body. Consult with the universe. Trust your intuition.

The Crescent Moon rune may emerge when you need to listen to signs and signals, when you need to tune your ear to the soft voice of the Goddess, or to your inner wisdom. It may emerge as a reminder to create ritual or to listen to the unconscious as revealed through dreams, intuition, and insight. It might encourage you to journey or to consciously engage in practices that connect you to the otherworld, to the mystery and magic of dreaming. It may be an affirmation of the wisdom you can gain by consulting with the runes and in being alert to synchronicities and messages from the divine. It may encourage you to stretch your own oracular powers and connection.

This rune also reminds us of the power of ritual. Of gathering together with intention and purpose and power, of raising energy, of sealing bonds, of linking arms in sisterhood and circle and solidarity. This rune calls upon you to create your own magic, to define your own truths, and to stir your own rituals into communal meaning.

You can do it. You already know how.

3: The Yoni

Rune of Making. Creativity. Fertility. Wealth. Pleasure. Birth.

This is a rune of creation. The womb of all possibility and all changes. The cauldron of life. Doorway, initiation, birth, and re-birth. Receptive, open, embracing. Fertile in her power and her purpose.

What waits within to be given birth and what wants to enter to be incubated? What nestles in fertile ground?

The Yoni is a hopeful rune, a joyful rune. One that reminds us to dance in the moonlight, to enjoy being naked, to delight in our bodies, and to celebrate the bodies, capacities and creations of others. This is rune of form. Of being formed. Of forming. This is a rune of fertile possibility.

Put your hand on your belly. What is waiting there in your pelvic bowl? What is waiting in quiet wombspace? What is hidden away, but growing bigger and bigger and waiting to be born? What do you need and what needs you? Take it to the body, bring it down into your pelvis. Sweep around the curve of the pelvic bowl and *listen*. What does she want to tell you?

This rune may occasionally bring up an uncomfortable feeling or some giggling. It may also make you grin with recognition and with fertile possibility.

This is a rune of *making* in so many forms. A rune of creation and pleasure and delight. It is an abundant rune, the wealth of your body, your pleasure, your creations.

What are you making? What is being nourished in your fertile dreams? What are you creating and birthing into the world? Is there something that wants to come through you?

Also, remember that birthing is not always easy, pleasant, and comfortable. There may be blood and pain and mess and tears in the process of bringing your creations into the light of day. Don't give up on what you are making, even if you struggle, because you will also feel the wild, sweet, relief of birthing something new into your open, joyful hands.

The Yoni rune may emerge when you are feeling

juicy and creative and abundant and in the flow of life. It may also show up when you feel dry and desolate and in need of creative nourishment. It reminds you to take pleasure in your life and works as well as in your body. It reminds you to create with wild ferocity and tenacious abandon. It reminds you to let pleasure ripple through you and to be born and reborn into daily miracles of co-creation and possibility.

Does your creative center need attention? Nourishment? Pleasure? Do you need more intimacy (or sex!) in your life. Sometimes this rune can be an earnest call from your body to pleasure yourself. There is a time to nurture and a time to be nurtured. A time to make and create. A time to receive and wait. Take pleasure in being alive at this moment. Take pleasure in the works of your hands and the sweetness of kisses upon your lips. Enjoy, stroke, touch, feel, engage. Honor feelings. Scoop it all up. Run wild with life, breathe deep, and smile.

Something is building to a climax and ecstasy awaits.

4: The Flame

Rune of Fire. Energy. Vitality. Enthusiasm. Amazon.

When you draw this rune, rest assured that *you can do it*. It is time to draw upon your deep, fiery, inner resolve. Let yourself ignite. Approach your task with enthusiasm and vitality. If that which you must do is not serving your vitality, either *do not do it*, or find a way to light its fire. Call upon your warrior, call upon your Amazon spirit. Step forth boldly, go forth with grand gestures and resolute purpose. At the same time, *dance.* Put on your body paints. Adorn your head and arms. Dance with your inner fire. Dance with your vision. Dance with your purpose.

How are you tending your flame? Feeding your fire?

How does your energy feel? Are you vital, alive, energized, and enthused about life?

Are you able to tap into your life force, the flow, the fire within, or does it feel silenced or shut off?

The Flame rune may emerge when you are feeling fired up and on purpose *or* when you are feeling wispy and tender, as if your flame is about to go out. It reminds you to tend to your own fire, to care for your own sources of energy and vitality and to remember that part of burning brightly means having a fuel source to draw upon. The Flame reminds us to keep our inner flames tended. Like other runes, it may show up in affirmation or encouragement or as a reminder that **this** is exactly what you need.

What do you need to thrive? What is feeding your fire? What is stoking your passion? What do you feel passionate and inspired about? How is your inner flame right now? How are you tending it?

Your enthusiasm is what keeps you going. Your energy is what brightens the world around you. Your fire is that which rests within.

It is hot, it is holy, and it feeds you.

5: The Heart

Rune of Love. Passion.

Right here, right now, *pause.* Rest, and know, that you are *so loved.* Held in love, supported in love, grounded in love. Draw it up. Draw it in. Breathe easy. You need not *do* anything. When you draw this rune, take a moment to acknowledge how often you act from a place of deep love. How underneath the surface of hurry and frustration and worry, there is a deep wellspring of love that drives you. And, in the next moment, extend your awareness, your grace and compassion, to recognize how often those around you also act from deep love. Love is the ground of being, love is the field of being. This love underlies your living and your interactions. Trust it, know it, be it. It is *inexhaustible.* It sustains you.

Heart-centered, breathing easy, step forward with courage, resilience, ease, and self-acceptance. This rune is also about love of **life,** that which is right in front of you, unfolding every day. This is *it,* this is real. Don't argue with reality!

The Heart rune also reminds you to take a turn to *receive*, to be nurtured, to draw in the love of those around you, to share passion, to remember to laugh. You can receive, you can give. Both capacities are boundless. Walk in love and love will continue to rise up to greet you.

What stirs your passion? What sings to your heart? What do you love? Do you feel loved? Do you feel passion? What moves you to your core?

This is a rune of love. It is open-hearted, open-souled, fueled by passion. When it arises, it may ask you to stand up for love, to stand by love, to be love. To risk for love. To set boundaries for love. To act for love. To withdraw for love. Let love be the center of your choices. Let her sing through you. Let yourself open in love, to love, through love. Be.

The Heart does not have to relate specifically to romantic love or human relationships, but may be about work, places, experiences that you love or things, experiences, and activities that fuel your passion and nourish your heart.

Passion. It bubbles. It boils. It dances and sings. It enlivens your spirit, it animates you. Passion. Juice. Energy. Roll in it, roll with it. Say yes. Drink it up. Laugh, revel, celebrate, create, harmonize.

Passion is the elixir of being and it speaks from the heart. Threading through your veins, beating in your chest, lightening your footsteps.

Embrace it and *smile.*

6: The Labrys

Rune of Will. Power in the world. Mobility. Having one's way.

The Labrys is a rune of assertiveness. Of standing up for oneself. Of claiming unapologetically one's place on the planet and in the stream of life. This is a strong rune, a steady rune, a rune you draw when the time has come to make decisions. When the time has come to say no. When the time has come to *choose*.

It is a rune of action, determination, energy, sustenance, vitality, and truth. It reminds us that it is necessary to speak up. To do what must be done. To say yes and to say no, without explaining, justifying, rationalizing or apologizing. The Universe is made up of many wills. Many wills joining, bumping into one another, dominating, submitting, sharing, giving up, being stubborn. The Labrys rune is about a strong, steady, inner will. A sense of personal power and the ability to stand in that personal power. The ability to step forward with purpose. To speak up with firmness. It is not about dominating or oppressing or submerging the wills of others. It can remind us of the power in partnership, in collaboration. Of the power found in working together, while still asserting one's own self-responsibility, potency and personal power.

The Labrys rune often turns up when it is time to make changes.

The time has come to draw upon your flexibility and your ability to notice what needs to be different, what is calling out for action and change, and to dig deep for the courage and will that are necessary to enact those changes. Remember that mobility can sometimes involve knowing when to *wait*. When to be still and when to return to something later in one's life course. This is a stubborn rune. It wants its own way. You want your own way. It isn't wrong to want that.

Have you been silent for too long? Have you squelched your own desires? Have you pretended to be something you are not? Have you expected others to read your mind and meet your needs for you, without needing to speak up? Have you been wanting to flee? Have you been wanting to quit or say no, but don't know how? That's where this double-headed axe comes in. *It can cut both ways.*

What needs to be pruned away? Watch out. She's chopping there. Be careful not to cut the ones you love, to cut off more than you bargained for or more than you want. Handle blades with care, for they can be dangerous. Is this what you worry about in asserting your own will? That you are dangerous? That people do not get what they need from you? That you are not enough? You are *more* than enough and sometimes that is scary. And, sometimes it scares others.

This is an assertive, decisive, strong, and powerful rune that encourages you to act without apology and to choose without regret. It is a rune of making changes and of standing up for yourself, of powerful will and of getting one's way. Where do you need to act? What choice is waiting for you? What change do you need to make?

The Labrys also encourages mindfulness in how you are "slicing" and how you are wielding your power. Do you feel powerful? Are you capable of asserting yourself? Of getting your way? Of moving through the world capable of getting what you want? Do you feel clear and decisive about where you are going and how you are getting there?

Where might you need to cut something off? Where might you need to pare something away? Where might you need to make a clean incision? What might need to be chopped?

While the Labrys can remind you of your own power and encourage you to be stubborn, it may also show up as a reminder *not* to be stubborn, to not be overly attached to getting your way, and to release or slice through attachments to how something must be. It may also caution you against cutting too deeply and reminds you to be careful not to cut yourself as you move through the world—being powerful does not mean that you must hurt yourself to retain power. Either way, it is a rune of sharp discernment.

Slice cleanly and without apology. Slice carefully and without regret. Remember to keep enough room around you to swing the blade freely.

7: The Dancing Woman

Rune of Power. Power from within. Strength.

Can you step into your personal power? Can you stand in your personal power? Do you know how it feels to do so? How does it look? How does it taste? What do you feel ripple through you? How do you know that you're there? Standing in power. Power in standing. Innerstanding. Understanding. Steady. Firm. Self-aware. Self-committed. Purposeful. Potent. Powerful.

There is nothing somber about this rune. It is unabashedly exuberant and confident and gracefully complete, totally alive. Perhaps standing in your power is what you need. But, perhaps *dancing* in your power is possible too. Singing in your power. Holding your power. *Being* your power. Inhabiting your power. Celebrating your body with abandon. Celebrating your mind and personality with the same. Honoring your quirks, finding compassion within you that stretches around you and out into the world.

The Dancing Woman asks: How are you standing in

your power? Dancing in your power? Singing in your power? *Do you feel powerful?* Do you feel like a powerful person?

Do you know what it is like to fully inhabit your power?

Do you move through the world with a sense of your own power or only in certain circumstances or experiences?

Are you afraid of your power?

How is your strength being tested?

Do you feel strong?

Can you let your strength and power ripple through you, wanting to be expressed, intensely felt, unapologetic and bold?

The Dancing Woman rune may show up in encouragement or in affirmation, perhaps when you need to be reminded of your power and to be encouraged to draw upon it, *or* as a celebration and affirmation of just how strong, capable, and powerful you are.

It starts within. It builds within. Then, it crests in a peak that ripples outward, impacting all who you encounter and inspiring them too: to step into their power, to stand in their power, to dance in their power. Power shared does not diminish, it expands, until each person can sing her own true song, drum her own rhythm, and dance for the heck of it.

Stretch your arms wide, open them to the sky, swoop them down and touch the earth. Feel it there within you. **You are a powerful woman.**

Draw it up, draw it down, draw it in.

Breathe with absolute certainty and clarity that who you are is *powerfully enough*.

8: The Box

□

Rune of Boundaries. Limitation. Stability. Lessons.

Boundaries. Hemmed in. Closed off. Boxed off.

Or...

Safe. Protected. Assertive.

How do you need to stand up for yourself? What do you need to speak out about? How do you own your own needs? How do you respect your own inner call? What do you want to do? How do you want to spend your time?

The Box reminds us of the critical importance of saying NO and how that relates to our ability to stay alive, vibrant, connected, and **vital**. In order to be of good service, in order to be strong and healthy, sometimes we will disappoint others, let them down, say no to good ideas, good projects, and even sometimes to legitimate requests for help. What does your body want from you? What does your soul want from you? What do you need? *Heed that call.*

Set firm boundaries, establish personal space, draw lines in the sand if needed. Women know, trees know, that boundaries must also be fluid and flexible, because that which cannot yield when necessary, snaps and breaks. Make sure that in your effort not to become taken advantage of, you do not become shut off, boxed in, and unable to connect.

We must forever balance the forces of separation and connection. Boundaries.

Where might you need to set firmer boundaries in your life? There are a lot of social messages to think outside of the box, but sometimes the Box is actually *exactly* what we need! It may show up for as almost a type of chastisement or reminder to set firmer boundaries, but more often it arises as a helpful reminder or reinforcement of what you already know needs to happen.

Boundaries. Lines. Squares. Diamonds. Protective forces. Sometimes with sharp edges. Sometimes with assertive language, but blessedly essential to wholeness of being and defragmentation of self. Sometimes we desperately need the Box. And, so we refine these boundaries, hone them, trust them, own them, and respect them, in ourselves and in others, when that is what our lives call out for.

The time has come to draw firm lines.

9: The Dark Moon

Rune of Wisdom. Door to the unknown. Crone's rune.

This is a foggy rune, a mysterious rune, a dark and knowing rune. This is the rune that holds questions that you're still learning how to ask. This is the rune that waits behind the veil. This is a rune of digging deeper, of twisting harder, and of asking more complicated *and* more simple questions and of being willing to wait in darkness for the reply.

The Dark Moon is a rune of honesty and truth-telling and truth-speaking and wisdom sharing, but it is also a rune that accepts fuzzy boundaries and imperfect and unclear understandings. It is a rune that recognizes limitations and honors rest. It gives permission for *not knowing*. It holds both. The speaking of your wisdom and the floundering in the darkness and confusion of your unknowing. It is the recognizing that wisdom comes in knowing how to ask the questions, not in always having all the answers. It is the rune of the wise woman, the sage, the crone, the ancient mother, the ancestral mother, the dark goddess, the deep within.

What do you know that you don't know? What secrets are you keeping? What is waiting to be brought from behind the veil? What is content to remain shrouded in silent mystery and phenomenal, wild grace?

This is the crone's rune. What wisdom is she whispering to you? This rune reminds us that wisdom waits in shadowy places, that the cave of darkness can be a cave of transformation and inspiration. It reminds us of what can be discovered in the dark of the moon, when no glow lights the sky and you must turn within.

This is the rune of cave time. Of waiting and watching and whispering and wondering. It is a rune of retreat, rest, and renewal. What can you learn from listening within your own shadowy spaces and wondering wishes? What does the wise woman within you have to share? Can you honor her? Where do you need to consult the Crone in your life, either archetypally from within yourself, from a real-life trusted elder, or from a crone goddess? What is waiting to be discovered?

The Dark Moon encourages us to look to sources of wisdom and to elders outside of us. What or who might you be able to learn from? Are you dismissing something or someone who might actually have treasures to reveal to you if you drop your own age-related blinders and really *see* them? What wisdom is right there, watching you, waiting for you, hoping for you, dreaming with you in the dark of the moon.

As I originally wrote this interpretation, I looked up and came suddenly eye to eye with a hawk in the forest for the first time…

You never know what is watching you from silent wings and shadowed, wild spaces.

10: The Wheel

Rune of Fate. Change of fortune.

What crackles in the leaves right under your feet? What stirs amidst the stones? What pushes up from cracked earth? What is bathed in the river? What cautiously creeps into the sunlight? What waits until the moon has risen to bloom?

Destiny, fate, fortune. You are not in complete control. You do not make all the choices. A million factors, seen and unseen, have gone into the unfolding spiral of your life and will continue to co-create it. You are a thread in the tapestry, a note in the song, a star in the sky, a drop in the ocean, a leaf on the tree, a cell in the body, a pattern in the sand. But, somewhere in the stars, your name is written and a sound chimes only for you. The tracing of your veins, the patterns of your fingertips, the gene patterns of your soulbeing. Is this fate? Is this destiny? Is this you?

You are woven by the weaver of all that is, held in the great, grand web of incarnation that encompasses time and space and everything beyond. The wheel turns, life unfolds, your breath moves in and out.

The Wheel turns. This is a rune of fate, but also of change. Perhaps some things are destined, perhaps many more are chance. Together, they form the patterns and process of your life. When you see this rune, it may alert you that a change is coming. Can you roll with change? It may be part of what feels like destiny. It may affirm or confirm something that feels meant to be. It may signal you that the wheel of your life is changing directions, taking a different path or a new course. It may also alert you to pay attention to the larger patterns around you, to the turning of the wheel of the year, to the passage of time, to the evolution of life cycles and stages.

A change of fortune may be on the horizon, a shift towards prosperity or luck, or an alteration in your own experiencing of life's rhythms and processes.

What is changing for you? This rune both calls our attention to changes in our lives and also to what is right here in front of us as it is, wild, wise, and wonderful. It is also an action rune, reminding us that we have a unique place in the wheel of life and need to "play our music." We can resist and push back, which can make things hard, or we can lean in and go with it.

How does the wheel of your own life feel right now? What might the wheel of the year be revealing to you right now? What pattern might you need to recognize? How can your understanding of life cycle stages and phases help you contextualize your experiences? What is changing for you? What might be rolling toward you or away from you? Do you need to get out of the way? Do you need to climb on? Is it spinning too fast, too slow, or just right? Do you perceive motion in your life? Do you feel like you're rolling along or do you feel caught or stagnant, without motion? What do you sense about destiny and fate and the larger forces that may shape or influence the pattern of your own life?

You are wild, wise, and wonderful. Don't waste what you've been given. Don't wait to play your music.

Don't wait. Roll. Roll with the wheel

11: The Pendulum

Rune of Patterns. Karma. Justice. Ethics. Trust. Conscience. Old patterns.

Stop making bargains with life, with yourself, with the divine, and let the pattern unfold and the rhythm emerge. What once was will be. What will be, will be. What is, *is*. It has been said that the arc of the universe is long and bends towards justice. Root yourself in an ethic of care. Trust that as the pendulum swings, tick-tock, tick-tock, it will eventually return to partnership, cooperation, and love.

You know you can trust yourself to do what is right. You know you can trust your own conscience and the rhythm of your own heart.

Which way is the pendulum of your own life swinging right now? Is it bending towards justice? Is it rooted in care? Do the outward expressions of your being reflect your deepest and truest values? Are you walking your talk? Are you living what you claim to desire? Are you doing it? Are you doing this work? Are you *being it*? Can you allow yourself? Can you give yourself permission?

Some people find that this rune can be a tricky one with which to connect, perhaps because it swings back and forth and is in constant motion. This is a rune of karma, of patterns, both old and emerging. Where might you be stuck in a pattern? Where might you take a step back to observe the pattern? Where might you be changing patterns and setting a new course?

The Pendulum is also a rune of justice and ethics. Something may be coming to a resolution, being settled, finding justice. What might be swinging to and fro for you? Where might you find unexpected insights from observing the motion? Trust your conscience. Trust your insight. Trust in your ability to navigate the patterns of your life and the world around you.

This rune may also emerge in a decision-making context—making ethical choices rooted in justice, trust, and a strong conscience. Consult with wise sources. Look at the broader picture. Let the fates and the muses collaborate to decide.

Take a deep breath. Open your hands. Drop your shoulders. Release your brow. Feel yourself planted on the earth in this moment. Then, ask yourself: *what do I know to be true?* In and out. In and out.

Thrum, thrum, thrum. You can hear it.

Pay attention. She's talking to you. Are you listening?

12: The Reflection

Rune of Surrender. Gentleness. Sacrifice. Letting go.

It isn't all up to you. Sometimes you have to step back and just let it unfold. Sometimes you have to bob in the current. Sometimes you have to crest with the waves. Sometimes you have to get battered against the shore, ground up into something finely textured and soft. Surrender isn't permanent. It is just part of wise discernment. When to hold, when to fold. When to stop, when to go. When to plant, when to harvest. When to say yes, and when to say no. When to float, and when to paddle.

The Reflection is a rune of open heart and open hands. This is a rune of acceptance and yielding. This is a rune of opening and releasing. This is a rune of letting yourself float, to be carried by unseen forces, rather than wrestling for and with control. Sometimes it is okay to go where the wind takes you, to drift with the current, to float out to sea, to give up and to be okay with it. Pay attention. What is asking you to let go? What is wanting to be freed? What is offering itself up to be sacrificed? What is waiting for you to unclench your fists and go with the flow? What wants to be released? What is waiting for you to open your hands, your life, and float?

It is time to open up, release, float, flow. What are you reflecting back into the world? Where do you need to sit and gaze into a still pool—of yourself, of nature, of your relationships?

This rune is not about giving up, but rather about *unclenching your life.* How can you soften, open up, release, and let go? Feel yourself expand into the delicious expanse of your body and the energy of creation within it. Bring your hands to your heart and belly, centered right here on this beautiful Earth.

Easy, easy. Gentle now. It's okay.

What are you releasing? Letting go of? Allowing to soften, release, change, flow, and float?

The Reflection rune may emerge when it is time to ease up on something. It appears when gentleness is needed—with self, others, life, or approach. You may see it when you are accepting a decision, making a choice, releasing a plan or idea. The surrender it requests is the kind of easy, mindful surrender found in releasing tension from your fingers and letting your hand trail through a current. It can also remind you that sometimes things might need to be sacrificed—sometimes with contemplation, sometimes without.

Sometimes the answer is just to *let it go*. No more forcing. No more struggling. No more trying. No more requiring. No more demanding. Just watching and waiting by the edge of the pool.

This rune may also emerge when you simply need time to reflect. Rather than being the time to make a decision, it might be time to just wait and sit, to see what eventually bubbles up. To turn things over without forcing or demanding. It is a quiet rune. A rune of ease, grace, and flow.

Somewhere in the quiet stillness of your own breath are the answers that you seek, the wisdom that you hold, and the knowing that is eternal. Unclench your fist. Unclench your life. Release, release. Let go and *float*. Smooth your brow, close your eyes. Inhale. Exhale.

Soften into the gentleness that surrounds you.

13: The Flying Woman

Rune of Transformation. Death and rebirth. Shapeshifting and change.

Becoming, becoming, becoming. Transforming, transforming, transforming. Unearthing, unearthing, unearthing. Being reborn, again and again. Isn't transformation the very *work of being*? The very work of the soul? The very fabric of thealogy, community, sisterhood, friendship, relationship, and personhood. Transformation: the core of life, the purpose of being.

What does *becoming* mean to you? Let it never mean you are somehow less than whole in this very moment. Each breath you take is a transformation. Each morning that dawns, holds the promise of rebirth. Each stone you flip, each page you turn, each word you type, it is all part of the fabric of transforming, becoming, changing. Change is constant. Sometimes change is scary and unwelcome. Sometimes you want to jump up and dance naked with it in the moonlight. You may want to hold on, to cling to something permanent, but the only thing that is really permanent is that unfolding, unwinding, deconstructing, deconstricting, unclenching, releasing.

The Flying Woman is a dramatic, energetic, powerful rune.

Things are changing, you are ready to fly!

What is dying for you? What is being reborn? What are you leaving behind? What is changing, being shed, cast off?

This is a rune of emergence into your full strength, full knowingness of who you are.

You may see this rune when change is needed. You may see it when something big is shifting in your life. You may receive it in affirmation or encouragement of making a big change. You may see it when you know it is time for you to embody Flying Woman, She Who Changes. You may see it as you move through a process of personal rebirth, as you give birth to yourself.

Let go, so you can watch what emerges. You can dance with her, sing with her, fly with her, cry with her, resist her, ignore her, embrace her, become her. *The Flying Woman*. She's ready to go. Are you ready? Can you flow with the tide and ebb with the moon? Dance at the edge of pain? Howl with potential? Respond to the rhythm played by your heart?

Join hands with your sisters, stretch out glad arms to the children, and then spin...

Spin together, in this beautiful, glorious, terrifying, magnificent, exhilarating, exhausting, amazingly eternal dance of life--in time, in space, in love.

14: The Cauldron

Rune of Alchemy. Temperance. Centeredness. Discipline. Art. Containment.

The Cauldron is a rune to turn to when you don't know exactly what to do. Take it all to the cauldron, stir it up, let it bubble, let it boil, let it percolate, let it stew, let it meld together with its companions until it emerges as something richer, deeper, more complex and flavorful than what originally went into the pot. Let it cook until you taste with spicy certainty exactly what has called your name, what awaits your flame, what sings your song, and what strums your heart.

The Cauldron holds a promise, it holds potential, and it holds that which you are already cooking. This is a rune of alchemy and transformation. What pieces are you holding? What can you contribute to the greater whole? What can you share with others? What flavor do you add to the mix? Bring it. Show up. Be counted. Do not be afraid to share.

This is a rune of focus and discipline, of centering

yourself deep within your body, of taking your thoughts down out of the mind and into your pelvis instead. What is she telling you? What does she want? What does she need? What does she know?

Sometimes when you don't know what to do or you're feeling overwhelmed or paralyzed by possibilities, you need to bring everything to the cauldron. Let it steep. Let it brew. Give it a good stir. Take a little taste. Decide what stays and what should be scooped out. What dash of zestiness is needed? What flavor needs to mellow? What could be combined to make a tastier, more nourishing, or more healing brew?

The Cauldron is a rune of containment and of alchemy. A rune of transformation and creation, but also a rune of keeping, holding. There is a paradox here—a rune of alchemy and change *and* a rune of holding and containing. What are you cooking up? What are you brewing? What needs time to steep? If you take your life to the cauldron, what will you learn? What will it teach you about holding and boiling and transforming and emerging?

The Cauldron is a rune of centering and of bubbling. Of action and change and also of waiting and watching, of stewing and brewing.

What will happen if you allow yourself to steep in

the cauldron of your own being?

When you receive this rune, something is waiting to be blended. Something is waiting to be dished up, something is waiting to be offered. Something is waiting to be created. **You** are the container for the emerging brew. *Get ready for the feast.*

Hold your promise over hot coals and watch it bubble into life.

15: The Whole Moon

Rune of Cycles. Moon energy and mysteries. Psyche's rune.

Cycles of life. Cycles of living. Cycles of love. Cycles of friendships. Changes. Growth. Some things blossom in the moonlight. Some things quietly curl up and retreat. Hope knows the mystery of the night. Our hearts know the mystery too. When we try to speak it out loud, it is slippery and undefinable. This is a rune both of paradox and power. Growth and decline. Effort, possibility, potential, and surprise. What mysteries are waiting for you in the light of the moon? What mysteries are waiting for you in the dark of the moon? What wants to be illuminated? What wants to hide? What wants to grow? What wants to decline?

Watch for the thin sliver of a fresh idea. Watch, too, for the fading crescent of that which has run its course. Reach out your arms to the mystery. Stretch them as a wide as you can. Stretch yourself as wide as you can. And, even then, know with joy that you can *never* embrace it all. This vastness. This void.

This grandeur. This dramatic sweep of time and place and power.

How do you make space to listen to your soul? What is she whispering to you? What are you not hearing or overlooking? Is there space in your life for the still, small voice of your spirit?

Are you in tune with the rhythms and cycles of your life? What can you learn from tuning in, from listening, from being attentive? Do you understand yourself as cyclical? Are you aware of the patterns and processes of your life or are they unconscious?

Do you pay attention to the rhythm of the moon? Take time to moonbathe? To listen to Her in the dark expanse of night?

This is a soul rune. A message, nudge, call, or song from your spirit to you. What does she want to tell you? What does she want you to know?

You may see the Whole Moon rune when you are feeling out of step with life and when you want to resynchronize, reharmonize with the rhythms around you. You may see it as a reminder to check in with the moon and with the other natural cycles of life. You may see it when you need a nudge from your soul's calling, when you need to listen to Spirit. You may see it when there is more to learn by simply being present, watching and listening.

Hold on. She ebbs and flows. The rest of life matches the tug of the moon. New things cresting, building, towering, standing tall. Then, crashing against the shore, pulling back, fading away, gathering strength and courage, and returning again and again.

It is time to listen to the whispers of your body as she is tugged to dance in the light of the moon.

16: The Serpent

Rune of Awakening. Kundalini energy. Cataclysm. Shattering.

Something has awoken, something has arisen, something is coming. Prepare for impact. Your world will be shaken and you will emerge anew from the splinters, like the phoenix. Shattered, tattered, torn away, splintered, crushed, broken. And yet, **there.** What's that? Something rises. Something with glittering eyes. Something with clarity of focus and vision and purpose and power. Something undulating, dancing in the rubble, climbing from the wreckage, lifting up joyful arms and open hands and saying: I'm ready. *Here I am!*

Shakti. Kundalini. This energy that coils at the base of your spine and unfurls through your throat and out your fingertips. *That.* That power, that vibrance, that potent aliveness. That elixir of courage. It lives in you. It walks with you. It waits with you to be unleashed, unfurled, spread wide, ignited. What within you is ready to awaken? What around you is ready to awaken? What are you are *not seeing?*

What have you been purposefully not looking at? It is time to meet her eyes. To taste her breath of freedom and to join with her in a serpentine dance of cataclysmic awakening and surrender.

This rune can feel startling, scary, or even ominous to some people, or liberating and exciting to others. It is a powerful rune. A rune of awakening. A rune of power and of shaking things up, dramatically, profoundly, intensely. The sensation of unfurling, uncurling, arising, *becoming* may be exciting and it may be scary and it may be both. This is a rune of expansion, growth, and change. The kind of change that rises up in full power and breadth and depth and asks *more* of you while at the same time helping you to become more. The power here is unapologetic, unabashed, unashamed. It is curled up, waiting for you, it is there, arising, it is unfurling, it is emerging. *Right there.*

What is changing for you? Awakening in you? Shifting for you? What is breaking down, collapsing, and then preparing to rise again? Are you in touch with your power? With what waits coiled within, potent, powerful, ready to be unleashed?

When you draw this rune consider what is arising in you. What has been curled up, stuffed down, or set aside, but is now ready to emerge, what is lifting its head from the shadows and is ready to meet the world, to be brought forth.

When you draw the Serpent, in addition to considering what is awakening within you, what *around* you is emerging? What might you be missing that is waiting for you to pay attention to it? What are you *not* looking at, whether intentionally or unintentionally?

Welcome, Shakti. We are ready for your shaking. We are ready to be cracked open.

We are ready to rise.

17: The Moon and Star

Rune of Faith. Inspiration. Truth. Psychic healing.

Hold to the hope. Hold to the vision. Hold to the healing. Hold to the vigil kept by your heart.

What do you have faith in? What does faith mean anyway? What do you know to be true? Where do you find inspiration and sacred calling? What fire is waiting to be lit within your own breast, your own home, your own community?

What do you have to share? What do you have to say?

Sing about it. Dance about it. Tell about it. Engage in deep talk. Deep thought. Deep commitment. Deep change. Deep healing.

The Moon and Star is a rune of uncovering. Of revealing. A rune of tapping in to that which already is, to that which you already are. To the potential that waits in your heart to bloom. To the passion that waits in your throat to be loosed. For the fire of creativity that swirls in your belly to be freed. Rune of inspiration. Rune of igniting.

Breathe deep. Breathe faith. You are guided. You are inspired. You are needed.

Trust the wild within. Touch the wild around. Breathe in the wild enchantment of your life. Touch it deeply. Feel it deeply. Hold it deeply.

Where do you have faith? Where do you need faith? Do you trust yourself? Do you have faith in your life, in the patterns it is weaving, you are weaving?

Where do you find inspiration? Truth? What inspires you? What motivates you? Where is your faith?

This rune may emerge when you need to have faith in yourself or when you need to have faith in the world, when you need faith in that great, grand weaving of incarnation of which you are a part. Faith in life, living, loving, and wonder.

You can trust yourself.

The Moon and Star may also remind or encourage you to follow your own star, to follow your inspiration, to be guided by inspiration.

Have faith in your own deep purpose, your own

deep potential, your own deep calling, your own deep longing. Be still. Place your hand on your heart and *listen*. The answers wait within.

The sun rises, the earth turns, the moon bathes the world, the tides lap the shore. We are carried by a great wind across the sky. We are a vital thread in the weaving of Life. An intricate and interesting part of a magnificent tapestry of Being in which it becomes difficult to distinguish weaver, web, and thread, so closely are they wound together.

After you've spent time in your own heart space, *open your eyes*. Take a look around, gaze at this bright, beautiful, wonderful world. Look at the smiles of those you love. Look at the memories that have carved space in your heart. Feel what comes welling up out of you. What must be said. This is your truth. This is your inspiration. This is your healing. It is also your gift.

May the moon and stars always light your way, for you carry stardust in your bones, and some part of you will soar on the wings of time forever.

18: The Sun

Rune of Healing. Rejuvenation. Recreation. Play. Radiance.

When you draw the Sun rune, you know the time has come to be healed. Not healing as in forgetting, or in letting go, but in accepting, opening, changing, and growing. An integration of difficult changes you may have experienced in life. Healing may be physical, it may be emotional, it may be spiritual, it may be relational. Consider in which ways you need healing and rejuvenation. In interpersonal relationships? Physical health? Emotional well-being? Mental health? In your relationship with yourself? In your relationship with your body and with the earth?

Healing is both *possible* in all there is and *available* through all there is. Healing comes in sharing silences, and sharing stories, and in sharing songs. Healing comes in creation, in offering to others, in opening your heart to a circle of women, in silence with another, in connection with your partner. It is also found in being playful and laughing together.

Where do you need healing? Is it possible that it already exists around you, ready to be sourced? Is it healing from within or without? Do you need to draw on your own resources or those of others? This is also a rune of play and radiance. Are you playing enough? Do you feel radiant?

This rune reminds you to enjoy the sunshine. To celebrate who and how you are right now. It reminds you to play and take time outs. What do you most enjoy doing? Make sure these things are not just reserved for *someday* or special occasions, but instead are a regular, enriching part of your regular life.

There is time. Healing is possible. Play is healing. Life is warm and full.

This rune also reminds us that **trying again** is always worthwhile. Draw upon the resources of the earth. Draw upon the resources of your sister. Draw upon the resources of your own heart.

In quiet spaces and laughing faces, *you will be healed.*

19: The Dancing Women

Rune of Celebration. Community. Shared power. Solidarity.

When you come together with your sisters, anything is possible. When you join with others in community, you can move mountains. You can build bridges and you can drum by the fire. When you listen to each other deeply, you come to know and be known, to understand and to be understood, to hear and be heard, to see and be seen. You are not alone. You are not isolated. There is a power in cooperation, power in joining hands, of linking arms, of connecting hearts, and forging paths together. Shaping lives in concert with one another.

Power expands when it is shared, it is not something that is in finite supply or that can be distributed by any one person. Power is within us and we must step out and into it, owning our own power, *inhabiting* our own power; fully and without apology, with grace and with firmness and trust.

The Dancing Women rune speaks of celebration and

community. Of joining hands in shared possibility, shared power, and shared creation. It is time to do more than just stand with your sisters, dance with them too. Abandon yourself to the joy of celebration with those you love.

If you feel a lack of community in your life, it might be time to create one. Instead of waiting for others to issue invitations or to create something for you, you do it! Send the call. Gather the women. Bring the people together. Create that which you are seeking and enjoy the act of co-creation, co-circling, and dancing with power *together*. Likewise, you can also *show up* for others—going to events, helping with projects, creating with others.

Do you have a strong community? Do you build connections with others? Do you struggle with power dynamics? Everyone can be power-full...together! Where do you wish to celebrate? What do you need to feel safe and connected within a group? Where are you waiting or holding back when you could be showing up?

Dance, sisters, dance!

When people come together, each standing in their own power, the power base multiplies and becomes infinitely possible. Many hands make light work, many voices make one song, many hearts beat together, many people stand strong.

This is a rune of uniting, of togetherness, of working, laughing, playing, celebrating, and journeying, with a shared focus.

There need not already be a path; walking together we create one.

20: The Great Wheel

Rune of Infinity. Completion. Wholeness. Universality.

Circularity. Wholeness. That which you seek can be found within you. And, in reaching out to those around you. Spaces, people, opportunities, deeds. It is *right there*, you need only look at it.

Round, curving destiny. Rough carved shape of being. Patterns hewn in places and people, speaking the language of community. You have what you need. You are what you seek.

My only prayer
today
is to touch
the infinite.

What is the shape of your life? What is the wheel of your life like? This is *it*. This is where you are right now. The wheel spins. Do you feel whole? Can you hold your center amidst the whirling of life?

The Great Wheel is a rune of patterns and the grand scope of life. It reminds us that the wheel of life is infinite and eternal. It may also be an indicator or an affirmation of completion—something has reached its end, met its destiny, run its course, been completed. It is a rune of your place in the great, grand scale of incarnation, the web of existence, the Universe Herself.

What is coming into being for you? What is being completed? Do you feel a sense of yourself in the greater pattern of life? Are you connected to a sense of destiny, purpose, and connection, and value? We cannot even begin to know all of the connections, patterns, and processes into which we are woven and within which we weave. Your potential is infinite, boundless. Your impact and creations are too.

The wheel spins, the world turns, the pattern weaves, your heart beats.

Your place is here, in the infinite spiral of life.

21: The Egg

O

Rune of Naming. Words of power. Magic naming. Communication.

The Egg is a rune of identification. This is a rune of differentiation. This is a rune of owning. Who are you? What do you know? What do you have to offer? What do you have to give? Own it. Do it. Be it. Try it. Say it. Know it.

Naming takes courage. Speaking takes truth. Story-sharing takes depth of being and clear vision.

The Egg is a rune of communication, clarity in word, thought, and deed. It is hopeful, it is helpful, it is magical, it is purposeful, it is conscious, *it is so.*

Listen to the world around you, speak words of power, ask for the magic names of the things that surround you. Listen deeply for answers to questions you didn't know you were asking, for perspectives you didn't know you needed, and for support and acknowledgement.

What do you need to name, to speak aloud? What needs your word magic? What needs to be honored with your voice or creative expression?

How might you need to communicate more clearly?

What do you need to speak up about?

What are your words of power?

How well do you know yourself?

Are you able to claim yourself, to claim what you need and can offer?

The Egg can also be a rune of new beginnings, of incubation, of starting out, of gestating, of change, growth, emergence, and renewal. What are you carefully holding in your cupped hands, guarding until the time is right for it to be spoken of?

It may show up when you need to speak up about something. It may emerge when you are hesitating to name and claim a part of your identity, passion, purpose, or path. It reminds you to "speak truth to power" and to define your life on your own terms.

It also reminds you to create a tender atmosphere for your own growth and incubation—to care about how, where, and what you are growing.

Carry yourself with mindful attention and care. Words have power. Choose them with intention and care. Speak clearly, kindly, powerfully, and truly. Sit in silence when needed and wait for the right time to emerge.

You will be heard in unexpected places, in unexpected ways, with unexpected allies, of time, place, heart, truth, and being.

22: The Sisters

Rune of Friendship. Sisterhood. Bonding. Promises and vows.

Reach out your hand to your sister, she's reaching back. Fingers touch in a moment of solidarity and suddenly you know that you have never been alone.

This friendship is ancient, wise, and deep and it crosses boundaries of time, space, culture, tradition, values and becomes part of the fabric of something eternal that women have been weaving since the first woman took the first breath. Some sisters come and some sisters go, some become entwined with you so that your paths and destinies intersect permanently in an unfolding spiral of becoming, exploring, learning, and knowing together.

The Sisters rune calls you to circle with your sisters, it calls you to gather the women, it calls you to drum, to dance and to sing together. It calls you to make ceremony and ritual and magic and celebration together. It calls you to comb out her hair, to place a crown of flowers in her hair, to wash her feet with love, to cry with her, to laugh with her, to sing with her, to celebrate her, and yourself and yourselves together. It calls you to make eye contact, to see her, to really see her, and to say, "I hear you, I hear you. Message received."

When you promise to be true to a friendship, you are promising to be true to yourself, as a woman on this earth. When you create ritual together, you are creating a microcosm of what could be, of what can be, of what is possible, and you are giving birth to what women's relationships and friendships can look like: whole, healthy, strong, accepting, supportive, honest, authentic, graceful, and real.

How are you tending your friendships? Are you keeping your promises? Do you have room for friendship in your life? Real connection? Deep promises? Do you feel a sense of sisterhood and bonding?

This rune may appear when you are craving friendship and connection. It may remind you or encourage you to seek true sisterhood. It may be a reaffirmation of the bonds and connections you have made or it may be a reminder not to take your friendships for granted and to tend to the bonds of connection with care and appreciation. In a less literal sense, this rune may emerge when the issue at hand relates to keeping one's promise or tending to any relational bond or commitment. It may also emerge with regard to a blood sister and your relational terrain with her.

Keep your eyes open, look for her. Don't be afraid to offer an invitation, a shoulder, a hand, or a song. Let her know she's welcome, let her know you're safe, let her know you're willing to birth something new together. Invite her in. Ask her to stay. Make her tea. Say thank you. And, be open to receive. Remember that relationships are reciprocal and you can give in healthy ways to each other.

This cord of sisterhood is eternal and strong, but it requires attention, dedication, honesty, and power to continue weaving the strands into deeper, more authentic connection and trust.

Listen, she calls your name. Go dance with her, barefoot in the sand.

23: The Seed

Rune of Waiting. Ripening. Pregnancy. Assessment.

Something waits beneath the surface of your life. If you listen, if you're quiet, you can hear her breathing. Stretching out, reaching forth. *Change.* It is coming. Peeking up from beneath the soil, a tender green shoot of possibility and promise, waiting to be nurtured. Do you have room for new growth? Are you able to water and tend to your dreams? Are you able to let light shine upon them? What in your life may be withering from neglect? What has attempted to sprout, but has been cut down, or uprooted, or malnourished?

She's waiting there… in dark spaces. Waiting to uncurl, unfurl, unfold, and *become*. This is a rune of possibility. A rune of deepest wishes. A rune of potential and promise. Something new is taking shape. Something new is waiting to be tended to. Growth happens in dark places. Change grows in dark spaces. *Life.* It is on its way. *Listen.* A seed is calling. What does she need? What do you need? You know.

The Seed rune suggests growth, literal, metaphorical, mental, emotional, magical. It is a rune of waiting—time is needed in the dark and quiet in order to grow. It is also a rune of assessment, of contemplating your options, your path, the avenues for growth and change. It can remind us that sometimes pushing through and up and out is what is called for, sometimes waiting in darkness for the right time to emerge.

What tender seed are you nourishing? What is getting ready to grow for you? What have you planted? What is growing for you? What has pushed up and ripening, preparing to bloom?

What are you waiting for?

What do you sense below the surface...of your life or in a relationship, commitment, or task?

The Seed is a rune of fertile potential, of development, of change. It also is a patient rune, waiting, waiting. You will know when the time is right to give a push.

This rune indicates that something new is taking shape. What seed dream are you breathing your life, hope, and deepest wish into right now?

What tender shoots are poking up from the

ground?

What needs more time to wait in the darkness?

What are you planting in the deepness? What are you beginning to grow?

It might be quiet, it might be soft, it might be tender, it might be private, it might personal. It may be something that is just taking root and it feels so tender and special and fresh that you don't want to tell anyone else about—just hold on to your seed dream and breathe your hopes into it.

The Seed reminds us that beautiful things take root in the darkness. This is a rune of waiting and ripening and is the perfect rune to consider during a time of processing and exploration.

It is time to dig in the dirt. Time to lie on the earth. Time to soak up the sun and be cleansed by the rain. Time to put down roots and send up shoots.

Put down roots, send up shoots…
Put down roots, send up shoots…

What are you growing?

24: The Tool

Rune of Labor. Production. Enterprise.

This is a rune of hard work. Satisfying labor. What are you unearthing? What are you digging up? What are you uncovering? What is causing sweat to drip from your brow, your cheeks to flush, and your heart to beat faster? This work can be dirty. It can be long, it can be hard. But, you can do it. You **ARE** doing it. Keep digging.

Remember too that others are doing their own hard work, unearthing their own riches, discovering their own treasures. What might you be missing in other people and how can you work side by side, turning over your deepness together?

Do you have meaningful work? Work that you love and that you dig into with enthusiasm? What are you working on lately? What is calling for your labor? What asks for your investment, commitment, and contribution?

The Tool can be a rune of encouragement to persist

and a reminder that hard work isn't bad, sometimes it is needed. Productive work can make you sweat, it can get your hands dirty, and it can satisfy like nothing else.

What do you do when someone undermines your work? Especially something that feels sacred to you? The Tool would advise you to keep digging, to throw your back into it. To keep sweating through it. There is always something to criticize in the world, but we have to be able to stand up on behalf of our own Work.

The Tool also may emerge when you feel like you're working too hard, as a reminder to gather your resolve and keep going. Or, depending on positioning, as a reminder *not* to let work take over your life. There is a time to be productive and a time to rest, and this practical rune focuses you on the work at hand. It can also bring you back to your Work in the world—do you know it, feel it, taste it, embody it? Your Work goes beyond the tasks and into spiritual purpose. It is your love song to the world, to the earth, to the community, a full expression of yourself.

This is a practical, purposeful rune. Put your heart into it. Dig deeper. Do The Work.

This rune reminds us that there is nothing wrong

with hard work. That often labor is required to bring something into the world. That throwing your heart, and back, into work is needed. That feeling the sweat on your brow is its own kind of lifesong. That sweating is part of life and growth and change and effort and accomplishment.

What is your work? What is calling for your sacred labor? Where might you be avoiding work that is needed? Are you willing to sweat?

The Tool can also be a wake up call if you are laboring too hard, too much, and you might need to give it a rest. To lay down the tools for a breather. Are you digging in the right place? Are you expending yourself in the right area? Are you working on what you really want to work on?

This rune helps us recognize the ebb and flow and heave and swell of energy. Life energy. Time. Perspective. There is a time and place for production, for being focused on the *doing* rather than the *being*. There is a time for rest and a time for stillness and the key is recognizing the differences between these times and not **forcing** what is not ready to emerge. Then, when the energy peaks, the shovel comes out and the digging starts. *Go with it.* Put your back into it, lift with your knees, bend with the wind. And, *dig*, sister.

Dig deeply.

25: The Winged Circle

Rune of Freedom. Liberation. Revolution.

You who carry wholeness within you, spread your wings. It is time to fly. What are you shaking loose? What are you expanding beyond? What are you rising above? Stretch those wings. Feel the quiver of energy pass through them. Feel your feathers drying in the sunlight. Spreading. Opening. Dreaming. Becoming. Lift them up. Test the air. Taste the sweetness of liberation. Take a running start, see the abyss yawning before you, and *soar*.

Soar beyond that which you thought was possible, beyond your capabilities. Soar, knowing that you are carried on a great wind across the sky. While the planet spins, the galaxy swirls, and stars are birthed, you are there, flying on the wings of change and inspiration.

Do you feel free? Can you expand yourself, stretch your wings, take chances, leap into the unknown? What are you liberating, shaking loose, unfurling? Where do you need revolution? What IS your revolution?

The Winged Circle rune may emerge in affirmation or encouragement of your own freedom of spirit or it may emerge when you are feeling bound or trapped and desperate to break free, to shake everything off and fly. It may show up when you need to free body, mind, or spirit from something that constricts you. Or, it may show up in celebration of the freedom you have claimed.

This is a rune of opening. Open opportunity, open possibility. Throw up the shade, draw back the curtains, take down the bars, turn the key, feel the lock click open, and take a running leap.
Liberation. Revolution. Shake off that which you no longer need, and *fly*. Fly free, stand tall, walk true.

Revolution keeps a steady tempo with your heartsong and the color of your wings.

26: The Cauldron of Reflection

Rune of Solitude. Retreat. Withdrawal. Creative solitude.

When you draw this rune, you already know what it is you need, what your soul is craving, and what you are asking yourself for over and over and over again. Time to spend alone in your own company. Rest. Reflection. Renewal. Retreat. Pull back, draw in, cocoon. It is time to come into relationship with yourself. To investigate that which you need to know from your own heartspace, your own soulsong.

What is crying out from within you to be heard? What creative impulse wishes to be followed? What heart message longs to be expressed?

The Cauldron of Reflection is a rune of creative incubation. What do you need to bring to the cauldron to steep? What will you cook up when left to your own devices? This rune is often a signal to draw back, to pull away, to retreat. To sit with yourself and see what you most need. It is a rune of thinking and pondering and considering. What do you learn in solitude? Do you have enough solitude?

When you feel the urge to withdraw or retreat, what do you do? Do you honor it, or do you push yourself to keep doing and going?

Conversely, do you spend too much time alone and need to emerge from the cauldron and come into the wider world to add your own flavor?

When you see this rune, you already know what it is that you need, what your soul is craving, and what you are asking yourself for over and over again. *What is that?*

This rune can be a gentle whisper from your soul. It can be an urgent demand for soul survival. It can be a reminder, a nudge, or nearly command. Each time, it urges you to listen well and wisely to the insights of solitude and retreat.

When you receive it, it is often time for conscious retreat and self-replenishment.

It is time to steep in your own knowing. Time to incubate your dreams, creations, and inspirations. Time to merge inner experiencing, to prepare a rich stew, a hearty brew, a precious potion, of your heart's desire. When you draw this rune, *pause*.

Rest. Take a time out.

Give yourself permission to take a retreat, to withdraw from external demands, and to sit with yourself:

Savoring your own flavor.

27: The Crowned Heart

Rune of Unconditional Love. Faith in love. Softening. Tenderness.

Open your heart as far as you can, and then, open it just a little further. Run your fingertips lightly over life, stare into its eyes. Breathe deeply, laugh loudly, sing joyously, be wild, be free, be love. If this rune brings up a tight feeling in your chest of *not knowing how*, it is okay, soften into that. Be curious about it. Where does it come from? What are you afraid of? What are you risking? Let your heart be kneaded by Sehkmet's claws until it is soft, pliable, flexible, open.

What do you love? Can you throw yourself wholeheartedly into love? Do you have faith in love? Do you love your life? Do you love what you're creating, have created, for yourself?

There is a wellspring of love beneath us, around us, that we can draw upon even when we feel most unlovable. Love is the ground of being. It is where we plant our feet, grow our lives, and love our loves. If your foundation is love, your faith grows from that base, underlying, nourishing, supporting all that you do, are, and have. Can you live it? Can you love it?

Do you have faith in love?

Deep breaths. Hand on heart. There. Do you feel it? You are loved.

There is risk in being this vulnerable, this exposed, in letting your heart crack open to your children, to your lover, to your friends, to the world, but it is through the cracks that light enters and transformation is born. Soft, soft. Open, open. Tender, tender. Careful now. *You no longer have to be afraid.*

Love surrounds you and you are an instrument through which its song is played. Make it a sweet one. Make it a long one. Make it a strong one.

28: The Tree

Rune of Prosperity. Projects. Plant life. Natural abundance.

What are you growing? What has taken root and is spreading as your legacy? What rich abundance do you offer to the planet? When you draw this rune, remember all that you *give*. Honor and celebrate that. And, remember all that you have been *given*.

Rest in gratitude and appreciation. The world is a prosperous place. The Earth is an abundant home. In the cycle of giving and receiving, it is possible for each to prosper in their own, healthy way. Stand firmly and feel your roots in deep, solid earth. Giving, receiving. Receiving, giving. In and out. Respiration. Inspiration. Prosperity.

We are the trees of the earth
our roots stretching deep and strong,
the stone of the firmament,
sister to the stars
that gave birth to the soil.

–Alma Villanueva

What are you growing? What projects are stretching their branches towards the sun? What is rooting in, taking shape, becoming abundant?

The Tree rune may emerge when you have something to grow. When a project is reaching fruition, when your work is thriving. It reminds you to source from the natural abundance that surrounds you and to be inspired by the wisdom, growth, and patterns of trees and other plant life. What can you learn from the trees in your life? Where might you be overlooking a source of natural wisdom, encouragement, and inspiration? Do you feel prosperous? If not, what would it take to feel so and what root or branch can you send out in that direction?

The Tree as a rune of abundance speaks of that which you are growing and offering into the world. We are all part of the great cycle of give and take, sharing and receiving. Does this feel harmonious to you in your own life now? Are you giving and being replenished at the same time? This rune also reminds us to rest. To feel our roots in the soil. To take time to appreciate being restored and renewed by the sun, wind, and rain.

Are you honoring your gifts? What are you midwifing into being? How are you being replenished? Are you tending to your roots?

The Tree asks us to take a moment to pause. Where are you in the cycle of giving and receiving? Is there something that needs to change?

Lift your arms to the sky and feel sunlight kiss your branches, transforming light to life.

29: The Pentacle

Rune of Protection. Holding. Maintaining. Sealing. Magic. Five Elements.

Earth, Air, Fire, Water, Spirit. Gather round, circle up. Call the circle, cast the circle, hold the space. It is time to call in the guardians, to ask for help, to protect yourself with the resources that surround you.

Protection. Containment. Safe space. Guard it well, hold it close, create it within yourself and in the environment around you. A circle holds steady. Linked arms are hard to pass through, linked spirits are hard to break.

Don't be afraid to say no, to guard your energy, to guard your safe space within. When you call a circle, let it be guarded: from negative words, pessimistic proclamations, or hurtful stories about others.

The Pentacle is a rune of union, unity. How integrated do you feel? Do you feel, sense, or experience the union of the five elements within yourself? This is also an rune of magic and working magic consciously, intentionally, and for a purpose. It represents protection and a harmonized integration and interaction between the five elements.

What are you committing to? Sealing? Protecting? Do you feel protected? How do you protect yourself? Hold safe space for yourself and others? Where do you draw lines and set limits and boundaries? When do you witness, when do you act? What needs your protection? What asks for your active energy of defense, maintenance, holding?

The Pentacle is a rune of holding space, of holding safe containers, of protecting others and oneself. It is also a rune of calling on the protection of the elements, of the magic around you. Is it time to draw a circle of protection around yourself? Is it time to call on your defenses, to raise a boundary, to seal a limit, to hold a line?

Serve as guardian to the terrain within your mind and spirit, as well as in your home, friendships, and circles. You carry protection and safety with you everywhere, whether you may call it up consciously or not, there is still a seal, a container, surrounding your own true self as well.

Earth, Air, Water, Fire, Spirit. Invite them in. Invite them to dance. Revel in the magic of this mystical, embracing union and hold it close to your heart. Guard it with your words, your actions, your thoughts, and your choices.

Every day is sacred.

We walk on holy ground.

30: The Two Circles

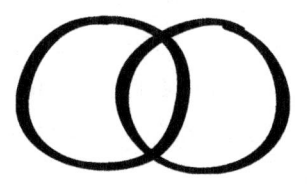

Rune of Merging. Joining or Dividing.

We come together with others in a dance of being so intricate as to be unfathomable. We enter their spheres, they enter ours. Linked, connected, drawing apart, cells joined forever in the overall body of humanity. Meiosis and mitosis. Separation and connection—always balancing these twin forces.

How are you connecting with others? How are you withdrawing? What is your dance of interconnection like? Of separation and connection? Of bonds and freedom? Of sharing and withholding?

The Two Circles rune reminds us of merging with others, of combining forces, lives, relationships, while also maintaining our own identities, boundaries, and being. Some things are shared, some are not. This rune may emerge when you need to connect, to reach out, to dissolve into harmony with another. It may also emerge when it is time to separate, to let the connection between you evaporate or to gently separate like the fibers of wool roving when gently tugged apart.

This rune may symbolize intimate relationships, but also other types of connections and interactions, including with your work, your tasks, and the nonhuman world.

Do you feel connected? Do you know how to separate? Do you wish to join with...*something*...? To draw apart from something? This rune may be your signal that it is time.

Recognize when sinking in to another is a thing of holy beauty and recognize when pulling away is the same. Holding hands, linking arms, forming interlocking circles of strength. A chain stretching across time and space, carried lightly on wings of eternity, and nestled, curled and connected in the womb of an ancient mother.

Interdependence cannot be denied. It is essential to survival and strength.

31: The Two Triangles

Rune of Focus. Analysis. Logic. Rationality.

When you draw this rune, the time has come to be **decisive**. To take action, to be assertive. To choose wisely, but to **choose**. Hone your senses, sharpen your awareness, laser in on that which cries out for your attention. Act with purpose, with determination, without apology. No excuses necessary.

The Two Triangles is a rune of action, intent, and clear purpose. You will see it when the time has come to make a decision, to act decisively, to be clear, sharp, focused, and intent. In combination with other runes, it may offer guidance on what needs focus or what to choose, but the overall message is twofold:

You must focus
You must decide

This rune encourages analysis, logic, rational

thought. It is not a rune of dreaming or feeling, but a rune of rational options.

Do you feel fuzzy or uncertain? Sometimes it is important to sit with those feelings and sometimes it is important to slice through them, to get clear and focused and to be assertive with your own powers of choice, action, and reasoned decision-making. Where are you having trouble making decisions or taking action? What needs your attention and focus?

The companion consideration that can sometimes emerge with this rune is that it can be a message of *discernment*. It may be time to ask yourself if you are being too focused? Would you benefit from taking some steps backs and letting your vision blur, softening your edges and your certainty and letting other possibilities arise. Are you letting analysis and logic dominate? Is your rational mind inhibiting you from a full range of vision?

This is rune of clarity and understanding. A rune with clean edges and sharp vision.

You are safe and connected. You are free. Make your choice.

32: Moonboat

Rune of Journeys. Travel. Out of body experiences. Astral projection.

What do I need to know?

She who travels. She who crosses thresholds. She who sets sail for far off places. Journeys can be inner or outer. Journeys can be solitary or communal.

What are you looking for? What are you seeking? To what end do you wish to travel? Do you wish to dig deep into your own soul? Do you wish to adventure across the ocean or into the sisterhood of community?

Where do you wish to go? Where are you going?

The Moonboat rune asks you to consider where you wish to journey—metaphorically, literally, spiritually. Do you want a communal journey, a personal journey? Do you wish to strike out across the country, overseas, or into your own heart?

How do you wish to energize your spirit? Where do you wish to travel? What journey are you taking?

The Moonboat is a call to adventure, a call to journey, a call to set forth. It might be literal, it might be metaphorical. It might be internal, it might be external. Either way, it is time to unfurl your sails and to set forth. Get moving. Take the steps. Make the move. Buy the ticket. Take the ride. Greet the opportunity.

This can be a rune of pilgrimage too, again within or without—where do you want to journey? Where do you need to journey? What is tugging at your heart and asking for you to set forth? Are you skimming across the waves or looking for a paddle? This can be a rune of moving beyond. Of moving forward. Of going. Are you ready?

Now is the time to take that step, to unfurl your sails, and set forth.

33: The Hearth

Rune of Nurturance. Domesticity. Caring for the home. Codependency trap.

This is a rune of hearth and home, of caring for one's space as a temple for one's family, of holding space for children and partners. A rune inspiring the creation of rituals and celebrations and ceremony for the members of your closest tribe.

The Hearth is a rune of caring, of giving, of sharing, holding, enfolding, rocking, and soothing. This is a rune of love and commitment and attachment. The ties that bind and the bonds of love and blood.

The shadow side of this this rune is the *codependency trap*. Notice when you use your family, your commitment to home and place, as a shield or excuse not to stretch beyond your boundaries, not to extend yourself, not to try, but instead to become complacent.

Be mindful of when you're expecting others to read your mind, be mindful of expecting others to refill your cup for you. Be mindful of trying to continue to pour when your pitcher is empty.

This rune reminds us to be priestesses of our own hearths. To nourish, nurture, and tend to those relationships that are most precious to us. To invest our resources, our time, and our love into our homes and families. How are you tending to the flame of family, friendship, home, and connection? Do you need to nourish this tender home base? Is something withering from lack of care, time, or attention? How does your home feel? Do you have a hearth? (It can be literal or metaphorical.) Do you feel like you have time to care for your physical surroundings, to tend to your home space? What does home mean to you? Is it a location, a feeling, people? Do you feel a call to gather at the hearth to nourish others, to tend to the heart of your home?

The Hearth rune may also remind you of the practical joy of caring for your physical environment and of the magic woven by everyday tasks such as mindful meal preparation and meditative dishwashing, the gentle act of combing someone else's hair, the pleasure of reading aloud to another.

The caution offered by the Hearth is about enmeshment—becoming so entrenched in your home role and responsibilities that you hold yourself (or others in your home) back from their dreams, that you let your caregiving become a cover for not doing something else that sings to your soul, of using your family and their need of you as an excuse to keep yourself small. The Hearth rune can bring up conflicting feelings—caring for hearth and home as your own home, your personal temple, but also the potential pitfall of using your home and family as excuses, or a cover-up for holding yourself back, for keeping yourself from what you could be doing, what you want to be doing, what you have within you to offer in the world.

There is a call for discernment here, sometimes the right choice is to focus on the hearth and to tend to hearth and home, and sometimes the right choice is to reach beyond hearth and home into the larger world and wider community. This rune can be a complex one to relate to, reminding us of the push-pull of the ties of blood and bonds, the twin forces of separation and connection, the ways in which we can mindfully and powerfully tend our own hearths and families and the ways in which this tending can sometimes become an excuse not to explore the other things we crave and also want to explore.

The Hearth challenges us to look at separation and attachment, of family and solitude, and those ties of blood and love that bind us to others relationally. How are you tending to hearth and home? Are you feeling bound or constrained by your home-based commitments? Is there something in your hearthspace that needs more of your attention and nurturance? How can you better tend to your home and those who depend on you? Or, where might you need to lighten up and let go?

How do our homes, our hearths, our families help us prosper, how do we have an abundant, fulfilling, prosperous life *together*. How can each member of a family help one another to grow, to thrive to prosper, to help one another reach our full potential instead of holding one another back in codependency.

Are you giving too much of yourself away? Are you able to make space for solitude and self-reflection? How are you tending to your hearth lately? Is there something you need to change in your family relationships or modes of relating to others?

Be careful, be loving, be kind, be open, be brave, be bold.

Link arms with your loved ones and head out smiling into the sunshine and the wide open spaces of shared possibility.

34: The Cauldron of Dancing Women

Rune of Honor. Loyalty. Commitment.

The Cauldron of Dancing Women is a rune of dedication, of steady purpose, of valor, of showing up, of trying again, of stirring together disparate elements and creating something rich, hearty, and true. This is a stable rune, a sturdy rune, a comfortable, solid, homing rune. It is a rune of sisterhood, of partnership, of community.

Stir with purpose. Cook with passion. Join with grace, ease, and dedication. Make your vows, set your limits, but always be on the lookout for the time to dance. Reach out your hands, join with others, make a vow you will not break: *to be true.* True to your friendships, true to your family, true to your home, and true to yourself.

We all grow within Earth's cauldron. Tempered, forged, mellowed, heated, combined, softened, nourished, transformed.

This is a rune both of containment *and* of action. The

Cauldron holds us, steeps us, allows our flavors to blend and mellow, and we are forged in its fires. There is an alchemy of creation in this rune as well as celebration, honor, and loyalty. When you see it, ask yourself questions about whether you keep your promises to yourself and how to show up for yourself as well as others.

When you see this rune, ask yourself how you are dancing? To what are you loyal? How are you committing your energy and your love? Do you show up in your own life with honor? Do you walk with commitment? Are you unshakeable in your vows?

How are you *showing up?*

The Cauldron of Dancing Women is also a rune of celebration. A rune of alchemy and creation and a rune of joyful connection. What are you creating with others? What have you committed to? Are you able to fulfill your promises? Is your word honorable? Are your actions, presence, connections, and commitment made with honor? What is calling out to you? What needs your presence in the circle, at the dance? What might you be able to create, discover, uncover, or explore in the company of others? How are your friendships? What do you stir into the brew of life that you create together?

What is transforming or growing, or bubbling in your links with others?

The Cauldron of Dancing Women may emerge when you are embarking on collaborative action. It may show up as a reminder that you are needed for some type of co-creative endeavor. It may be found when you need to be reminded of the power of your own presence, your own ability to show up for others. And, it may arise as a cue, reminder, affirmation, or encouragement of your own honor, of acting, speaking, creating, and *being* with honor in your life.

This is both a joyful rune and a serious rune. When you link hands with another, do so with great love, great courage, and great commitment.

Be alert for what is bubbling, for what is ready to be served, for what is ready to be savored together.

35: The Broom

Rune of Purification. Clean sweep. Cleansing.

This is a rune of new beginnings, of starting over, of new possibilities, of sweeping out dusty corners of minds, hearts, and lives. Of flinging open the windows and letting in the sunshine. Of spreading arms in welcome and of laughing with freedom and joy.

Uncover. Turn over. Declutter. Clean sweep. Blank slate. Swipe it away. Clean it out, clear it away. And then, *you're ready.*

With purification comes change and possibility. Hope and power. Peace and freedom. Keep sweeping. Be whole.

The Broom can be a very practical and direct rune—i.e. what do you actually need to declutter and clean out of your physical living space? And, it can also be metaphorical, asking you to consider what old thought patterns or habits need to be unwound from your brain and cleared away. Either way, this rune asks you to pick up your broom and go looking, prepared to sweep in all the corners. Don't be afraid, you can clean it away and start from a place of freshness.

This practical rune often shows up in a practical way, such as when you are in the mood for spring cleaning or for decluttering your home. This is a rune of new beginnings, of cleaning out, sweeping away, and wiping off the dust, whether literally, or in the dusty corners of your mind where tired old thought patterns replay. What needs to be released, cleansed, purified, or freed in your own life? Where is your energy stuck or dusty? Where do you need to sweep?

Do you really need to clean something out, up, or away? Do you need to declutter, unload, remove possessions? Or, do you need to clear out old patterns and habits, thought processes, unwelcome experiences? The Broom may indicate a need to make a clean sweep, to start over, to begin again. What you might need to purify or cleanse for yourself?

Sometimes this rune emerges when you actually need to remove something from your life—it might be a relationship, it might be a habit, it might be a possession or collection, it might be a tradition that is no longer working, it might be a job, a location, or a commitment.

What are you sweeping out, whether physically, emotionally, or metaphorically?

What is in the closets or under the beds that needs to be investigated and swept away? What cobwebs are draped from corners of your mind, wound around your heart, laced through your pelvis, twined through your brain, in ways you might not even fully comprehend? What needs to be released, let go, purified, cleansed?

Don't be afraid, pick up your broom and go looking. Turn over all the rocks, look in all the corners, dust down all the cobwebs.

Lay on the earth with your arms spread in the sunshine and know that you are whole. You are loved. You are powerful.

36: The Spiral

Rune of Initiation. Rites of passage.

This is a journey rune. Spiraling rites of passage, opened doorways, surrendered moments, grace and struggle in changes, hopeful pauses, liminal places, threshold moments, and leaps of faith.

When the Spiral rune is drawn, ask yourself: how have you celebrated transitions? What rites of passage are you preparing for? What initiations are awaiting you? What sacred work calls your name? To what holy purpose will you be dedicated?

Initiation is a path and a process, not a single discrete event. Rites of passage mark transitions from one point to another on a continuously unfolding spiral of time, person, and space. One's *whole life* can be a process of initiation; initiation into your own existence.

Who are you? Who can you be? What holy flame speaks your name? What task ignites your heartsong? What place awaits your visit? What people hunger for your touch?

Life is an initiation. Life moves in spirals and circles, not in straight lines. Where are you on your sacred path? What is unfolding for you? Do you feel lost along your way? Are you feeling your way through darkness or skipping along a clear path in the sunshine? What are the key initiatory moments of your life? What smaller, less culturally recognizable transitions, rites of passage, or initiations have you been through, are preparing for, or are currently engaged in?

Initiations can be quiet moments or big events. They can be celebratory or painful. You may feel like you've been dragged through these passages by your fingernails, or carved your way through rock with sheer will, or like you've been swept along on waves of joy. There may be ceremony and song. There may be weeping. There may be community or solitude, but travel you will, through the gateways of change, and along the unfurling path of your own sacred story.

The Spiral often appears to remind us that life involves an unfolding spiral of initiatory moments. This rune may also appear with regard to someone else's rite of passage, initiation, or sacred path. You might see it in the context of guidance or mentorship, you may see it as a signal or sign that you are on the right path. It may indicate that you are helping others with their significant life transitions and be a call to, or affirmation of, the sacred work of ceremony creation to honor life's key moments. The Spiral may encourage you to unfurl, to uncurl, to share your stories, and your personal journey with others. It is about moving forward, dipping back, walking, crawling, running, skipping, and dancing as you move through the folds of your being,

This is the rune of initiation. This is the rune of change.

It is time for dedication to your sacred path.

37: The Wand

Rune of Blessing. Making sacred. Honoring. Calling in. Sending forth. Marking boundaries. Consecration. Blessing.

Destiny is knocking and ready to link hands with yours. Pick up your wand, claim your birthright, your power and your destiny. Step out with strength, confidence, and flow. Mark your boundaries without apology or hesitation. Cast the circle, consecrate your heart. Know your body as a temple, your person as an offering, your spirit as a gift.

Cast a circle with your breath. Plant your feet firmly on solid ground and draw up the ancient wisdom that waits for you. Let go of that which holds you back, open wide to embrace that which calls your name, whispering from deep, secret places, from bright, shining spaces, and from quiet corners of your soul.

Name it, bless it, be it, do it, hold it, know it, live it.

It is time to call in that which you need and offer out

that which you have. Giving, receiving, giving, receiving, like the very breaths you take upon this earth. Honor the pulse of blood through your veins, the sparkle of ideas through your mind, the breath filling your lungs, the energy that moves you forward.

The Wand rune is about both calling in and sending forth. What are you drawing to you, bringing in, attracting to you? What are you putting forward? How are you blessing your life, the people, places, and things of your world? It is important to remember that we can't call in what we're unwilling to send out. This is a rune of both actions—of calling it in and of sending it out. There is an intimate relationship between the two.

The less immediately visible aspect of the Wand is the marking of boundaries, the holding of safe space, of demarking holy ground, and establishing borders. A wand can be used to cast a circle, to mark a safe space, to protect, in this act of blessing, an act of protection and boundary marking and identifying. In the book *The Twelve Wild Swans* by Starhawk and Hilary Valentine, they describe boundaries as both your own edge as well as the sensory system that identifies the edges of others. How are your boundaries? Are you able to hold your own perimeter while still being permeable and flexible when needed?

What is sacred to you? How do you honor it? What are you consecrating with your touch, your breath, your vision? How do you sense the sacred?

You might experience this rune as a simple affirmation, a nod, to the blessings you are sharing with others, the rituals you are guiding, the magic you are co-creating, the passages you are honoring. It might also remind you that you need to call something in, that you need to honor the sacred—whether your own sacred work or something sacred to you. It might remind you to be grateful for the blessings in your life, or it might inspire you to call on the forces that surround to consciously create a blessing, an event, an experience, a sacred space, or something you need.

Honor, bless, dedicate, consecrate. Hold deep knowing of the inherent worth and value of that which is within you and around you.

Hold yourself, hold the vision, hold the truth, hold the power.

Wave your wand in blessing, in dedication, in honor.

38: The Sun and Moon

Rune of Laughter. Joy. Ease. Poise. Hilarity. Belly laughter. Pure fun. Healing laughter. Baubo's rune.

When you draw this rune, take a minute to put down anything else you are carrying, doing, or thinking about. Let your shoulders relax and release. Let the breath move easy down into your belly. Then *smile*. Smile from your roots up through your branches. Feel joy suffuse you, filling you, bathing you, and *laugh*. Laugh from your belly. Laugh from your heart. Laugh with the wild abandon of *freedom* and release.

This is a rune of letting go. This is a rune of release and freedom. This is a rune of trusting oneself and what makes you smile. *Are you afraid to laugh?* Are you scared to let go? Do you fear the loss of control that comes with hilarity? It is time to shake that off. Don't be afraid. Laugh, sister, laugh. It is time to have some *fun!*

When was the last time you truly laughed?

Are you able to let go and feel joyous and free?

What makes you laugh?

When do you have the most fun? How can you invite more fun into your life?

When, where, why, and with whom do you laugh the most? Are you experiencing enough of those places, people, and experiences.

The Sun and Moon rune is the most joyous, delightful rune in the system. You may receive it as a reminder to let go and roar with laughter *or* as an affirmation that being lighthearted, joyful, and responding to life with laughter is the best response.

Know that you are as free as you allow yourself to be.

39: The Winged Heart

Rune of Ecstasy. Transcendent state. Peak experience. Orgasm. Union with all. Awe. Union with Goddess. Out-of-body.

How often do you *think* instead of *feel*? How often do you hold something in your mind rather than feel it in your body? Do you know what ecstasy feels like? Can you allow yourself to experience transcendence, awe, a peak of oneness? Do you know what it is like to have pleasure fill your body, rippling through you and out of your fingertips until you have become a part of the great, seamless, beautiful tapestry that Life is weaving all the time, whether you pay attention or not? Can you spread your arms and sink into the very body of the Goddess?

Close your eyes and let go, melting into Her, dissolving control. Releasing, releasing, releasing, until there is nothing left but pure sensation and awe.

Adjust your life, your expectations, and your grasping until ecstasy becomes a regular part of your living and being. This is your birthright, not a one-time treasure, but an awareness to be lived and regularly played with, touched, smelled, tasted, felt.

Dive in. Let it roll over you. Let it sweep you away on the wings of passion and delight.

Set it free. The Winged Heart is a rune of ecstasy and connection. Of being fully immersed in pleasure. Of being flooded with awe. It is a rune of divine union, a truly liberating, transcendent, ecstatic, complete sensation of life in the hand of the goddess. You are capable of profound connection. You can love it. You can flow with it. You can fly with it.

This rune also may encourage you to trust to your heart—that it can take you higher and deeper than logic might dictate.

Do you know what awe feels like? Can you be present with awe? Daily awe? Is there something that needs you to step into it, to be present with it, to enfold it with your wings of love?

This is a full-bodied, full-throated, full-hearted celebration of life.

When this rune is drawn, you know it is not the time for holding on, for standing steady, for grounding, for digging in. It is time for expansion, for ripples of joy to flood you. Time to be swept away, carried away, freed. Flying. Ecstatic. Alive.

It is time to soak your heart in the streams of change, the ocean of possibility, and the arms of All That Is.

There is nothing to lose and everything to gain.

40: The Veil

Rune of Mystery. Sound of silence. Revealing. Concealing. The Unknown. Not time for answers. The wishing rune. Isis veiled or unveiled.

What do you see when illusions fall away? When pretensions and old habits crumble to dust? Mystery. Shrouded. Waiting. Concealed. Do you have enough strength to pull back the curtain? Can you gaze into the heart of mystery? To look at what lies in wait. What has been concealed, hidden, put away for so long. What have you hidden? What do you keep concealed? What do you veil from the world?

Some things belong to the sacred mystery, never able to be confronted directly. *Can you hold the space for the ever-unknown as well?* For not knowing. For no answers. Can you hold the hope for that?

What is happening in your inner temple? What remains when everything you don't need has fallen away? What will you see when you drop the curtain and fully examine your own life? What hope waits in shadows? What love is veiled? What are you seeking?

This rune reminds us that sometimes the answers we seek can seem hidden from view. And, that the guidance we seek, the questions we ask, may be met with silence. *Silence is sacred and within it rests infinite possibility.*

The challenge and gift in this rune is the not knowing. It is not the time for answers. It is time to sit behind the curtain, wondering. That's okay. This is a shadowy, veiled rune that might be uncertain or even frightening, or it may give you permission to sink back into the arms of mystery, to rest for a time in the wild unknown, in the blind space of not knowing. Just wait. This can be a rune of revealing as well, of dropping the curtain. Or of drawing up the curtain and feeling content to not know for now.

There is a peace within the sound of silence. A lot can be heard while waiting behind the veil. A forgiveness and a blessing in the mysterious waiting spaces in our lives.

Inhale.
Exhale.
Wait.
Watch.

Wonder.
Learn.
Reveal.

What do you know you don't know? What are you waiting for? What is waiting to be discovered or revealed? Can you sit in and with the not knowing? What do you hear in the silent mystery? Are you feeling impatient or pushy or anxious about something? What might happen if you let it remain unknown or hidden?

Take a deep breath and *wait*. That which is concealed will be revealed. That which is unknown will become known. That which is unanswered will become answered. And… arising in an endless chain will be new questions, new mysteries, and new possibilities… waiting behind the curtain.

Make a wish. It is time to find your answers in that which is *unknown.*

What is fuzzy, out of focus, distant, shrouded, glazed, covered, secretive, lurking, dancing around the edges of your vision, dancing around the edges of your consciousness, and dancing delicately through your dreams? What is that? What *is that*?

Lift the curtain.

Rune Layouts

Daily Guidance

The most basic use for Womanrunes is for daily guidance. Sift through the runes or shuffle the cards gently while focusing your thoughts. Take some deep breaths, center yourself in the present moment, and still your mind. When you feel ready, draw a rune and see what it says to you. If you don't recognize the rune automatically, look up its name and then, "let your mind wander around it, and see what associations crop up. Out of this process you should be able to come upon relevant insights that will help to answer your question" (Mountainwater, *Womanrunes* booklet, p. 22). It will also shed light upon issues at hand, whether spoken or unspoken. Another method is to simply open the book at random and see which rune wishes to speak to you.

Drawing a Womanrune as your message or guidepost for the day can be a powerfully centering experience that focuses your thoughts and brings you into clarity for the day to come.

For all runing possibilities included, use your own intuitive understanding first and then draw upon the additional interpretation information in this book.

Note: for all the layouts themed around specific runes you may wish to remove the title card from the deck before drawing your runes for the layout.

In Shekhinah's words: *"the main thing to remember with any divination process is that your inner voice knows best. To make contact with this deep part of yourself, it helps to create a ritual setting and make yourself quiet, relaxed, and focused. The more you concentrate on the process, the more successful you will be.* **Listening to the deep self is a skill that can be developed like any other..."** *(p. 23).*

Messages from Womanrunes are not prescriptive or directive, instead they serve as a dynamic conduit to exactly what you need to hear and receive in that moment. When you use them for a longer term question or an annual oracle, remember that they are not intended to *predict* the future, but rather to bring your awareness to themes, issues, or messages that are calling for your attention.

Basic Three Rune

After following the initial centering process, draw three runes and lay them out in a row. The first rune represents the past and its relationship to your current issue or question. The second represents the present. The third represents the future and what you need to know as you move forward.

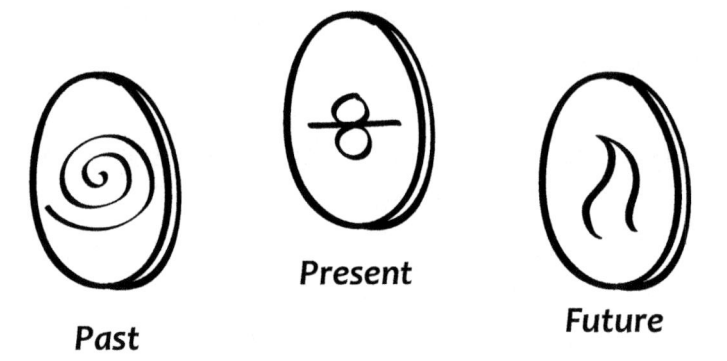

Past

Present

Future

The Crone Throw

This layout is based on one described in the book Crone Stones by Carol Lee Campbell (www.cronestones.com).

After focusing your thoughts and centering your body and breath, choose three runes and lay them out left to right.

The first rune is the **Maiden** rune. *It reveals your potential in the situation.*

The second rune is the **Mother** rune. *It tells your outcome to the situation.*

The third rune is the **Crone** rune. *It is your explanation of how to achieve the first two runes.*

(Crone Stones manual, p. 67)

Maiden

Mother

Crone

Shekhinah's Layout
(reprinted from the original Womanrunes booklet, p. 25)

Meanings:
1. **Self:** identity, personality, self-image, current feelings, attitudes, situations.
2. **Relationships:** love matters, interaction, intimacy, partnerships, family, friends.
3. **Environment:** living space, workspace, surroundings and their influences.
4. **Immediate past:** recent occurrences and energies.
5. **Immediate future:** upcoming occurrences and energies.
6. **Healing:** health matters, sources of healing, what needs healing.
7. **Livelihood:** career, money, survival, work.
8. **Deep past:** childhood, long-range past, past lives, roots of personality.
9. **Wild rune:** random energy, surprises, possibilities, tendencies.
10. **Magic:** spirituality, religion, psychic matters, the soul's journey.
11. **Change:** influences of and for change, transformations; that which is changing.
12. **Wish rune:** hopes, dreams, expectations, projections, fears.
13. **Outcome:** probable future, culmination of the runes.

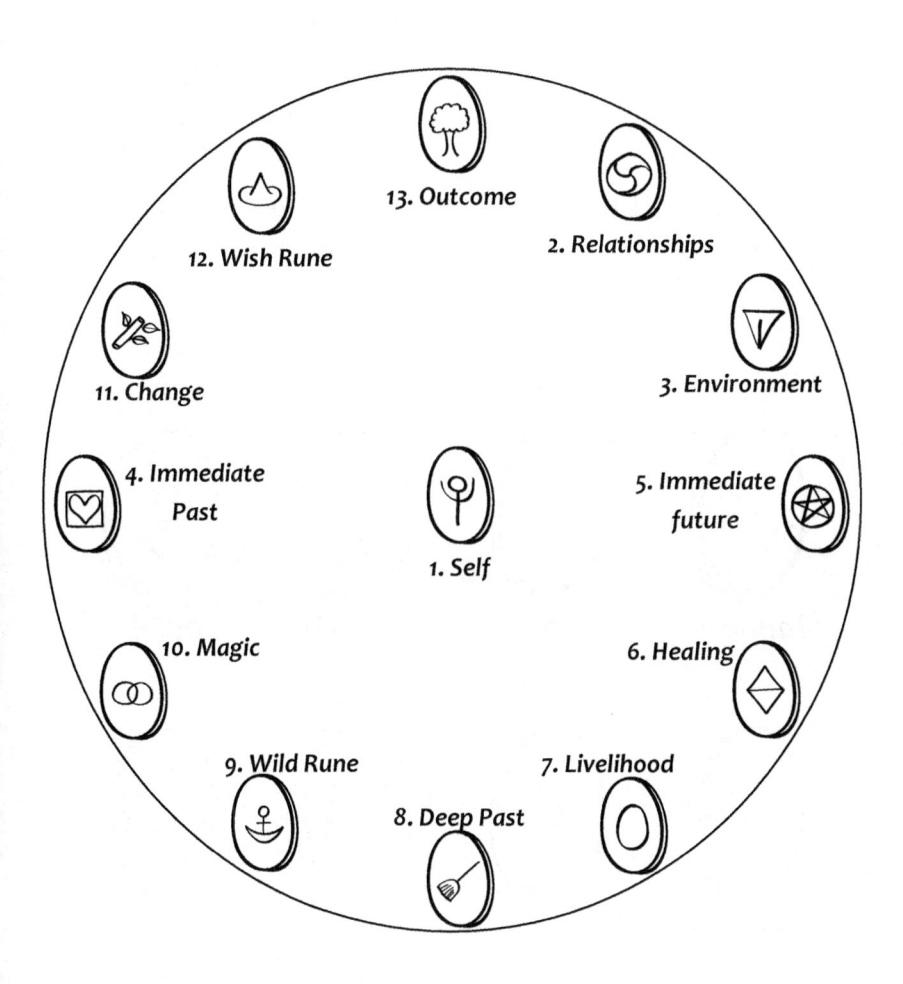

13. Outcome
2. Relationships
12. Wish Rune
3. Environment
11. Change
4. Immediate Past
1. Self
5. Immediate future
10. Magic
6. Healing
9. Wild Rune
7. Livelihood
8. Deep Past

Annual oracle

In January of the new year, set aside some time, energy, and focused ritual space to draw an annual oracle for yourself for the year to come. Draw 12 runes and lay them out, one for each month of the year. Record the symbols and their basic message on a grid for an overview of the upcoming year. Refer to the grid for ongoing guidance throughout the year.

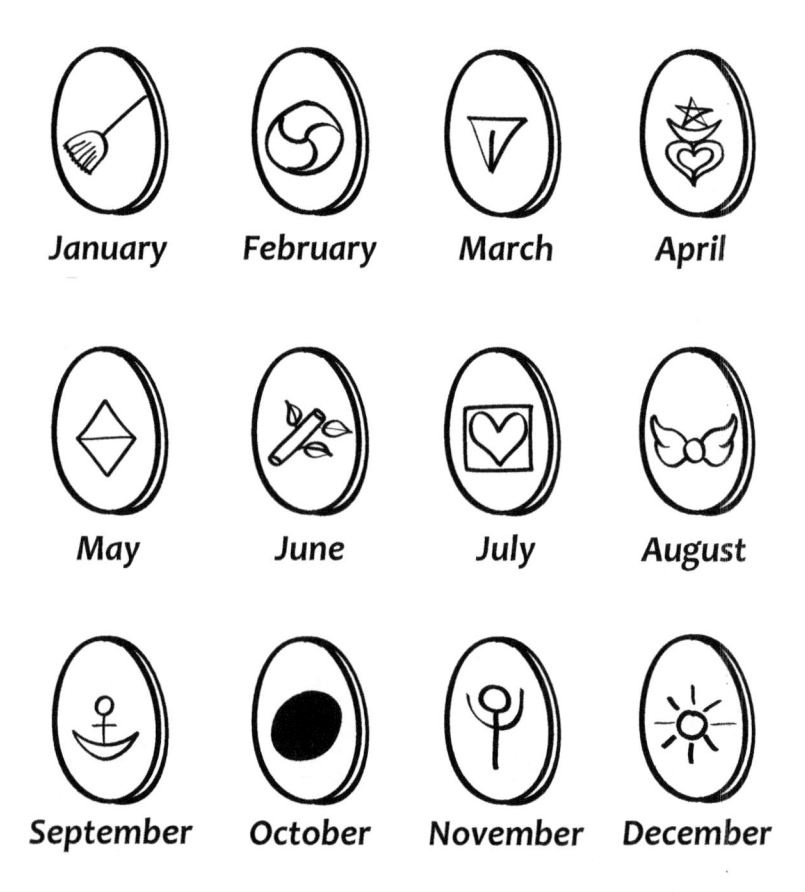

January	February	March	April
May	June	July	August
September	October	November	December

Annual oracle variation

(adapted from my favorite tarot deck, The Gaian Tarot by Joanna Powell Colbert, p. 262. http://www.gaiantarot.com/)

Draw seven runes at the beginning of the new year and lay out as illustrated. As with other layouts, take a few moments to sit with the entire layout and intuit its overall pattern and message before moving on to specific interpretations. Basic correspondences for this layout are as follows:

1. What do I leave behind in the old year?

2. What do I open up to in the new year?

3. Key opportunity of the new year.

4. Key challenge of the new year.

5. Hidden concern (this rune should be pulled from the bottom of the deck).

6. Deep wisdom/advice from goddess.

7. Key theme of the new year.

If you keep a record from year to year, the following year use the last rune from the preceding year (7) as the first rune in the next year's layout.

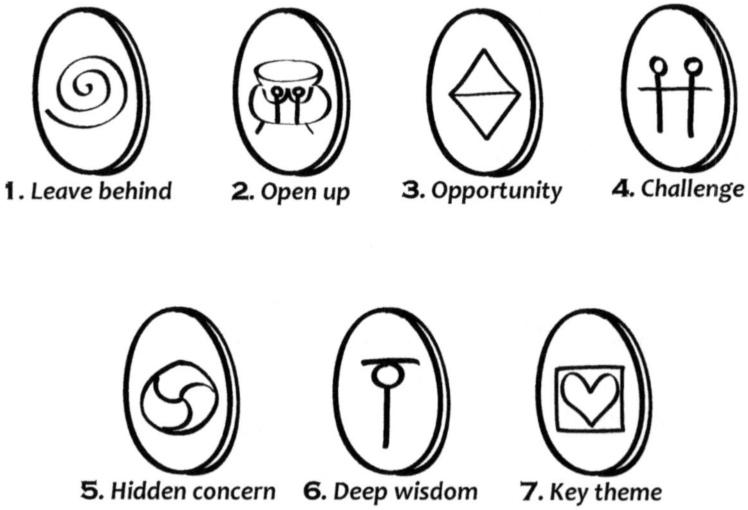

1. Leave behind   2. Open up   3. Opportunity   4. Challenge

5. Hidden concern   6. Deep wisdom   7. Key theme

The Whole Moon

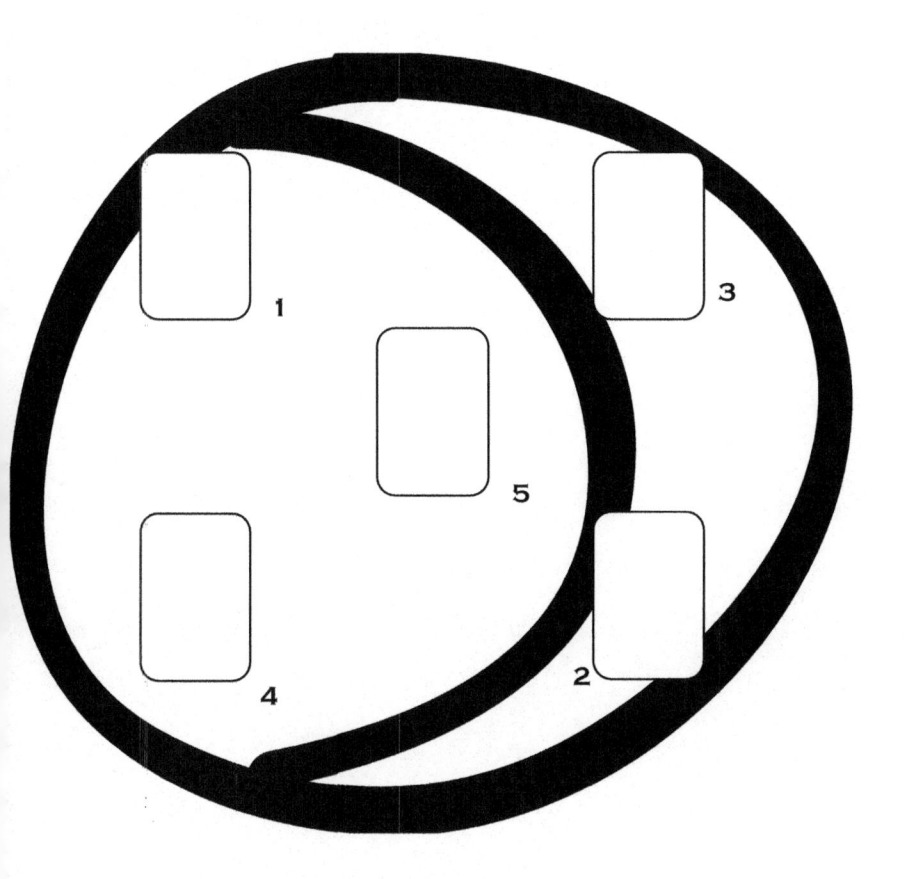

1. **Growing**: what is changing, blossoming, or being illuminated?
2. **Declining:** what has run its course and is fading away?
3. **Fresh idea**: maybe a thin sliver for now, but beginning to dance in my awareness...
4. **Whispers** of my body and her rhythms
5. **What does my soul need?**

The Crescent Moon

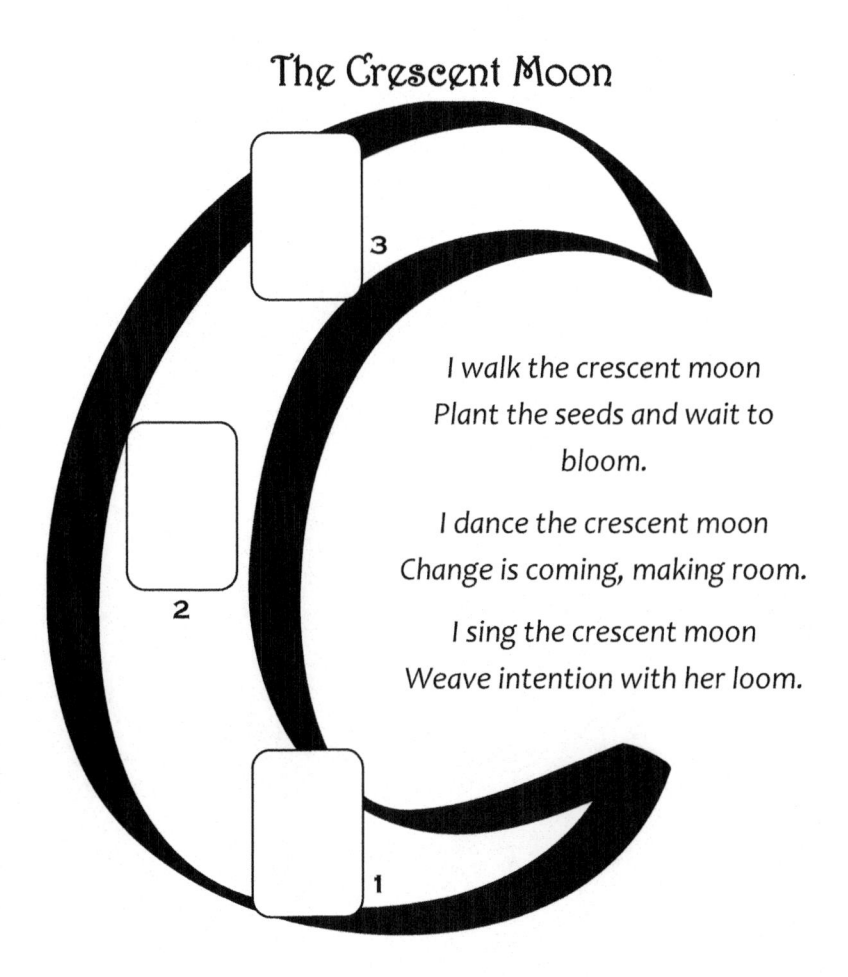

*I walk the crescent moon
Plant the seeds and wait to bloom.*

*I dance the crescent moon
Change is coming, making room.*

*I sing the crescent moon
Weave intention with her loom.*

1. **Planting:** What seeds am I planting? What am I incubating or preparing to grow?
2. **Making room:** What is changing? How am I making room?
3. **Weaving:** What is working through me? What is my intention or focus point?

The Seed

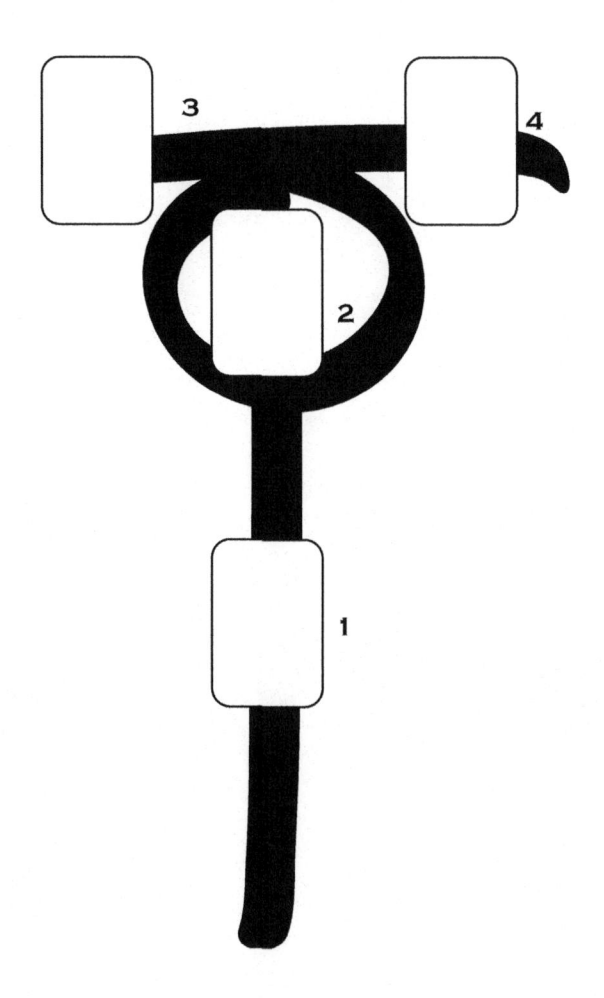

1. What is waiting in the darkness?
2. What is ready to emerge?
3. & 4. What do I need to know as I grow?

The Cauldron

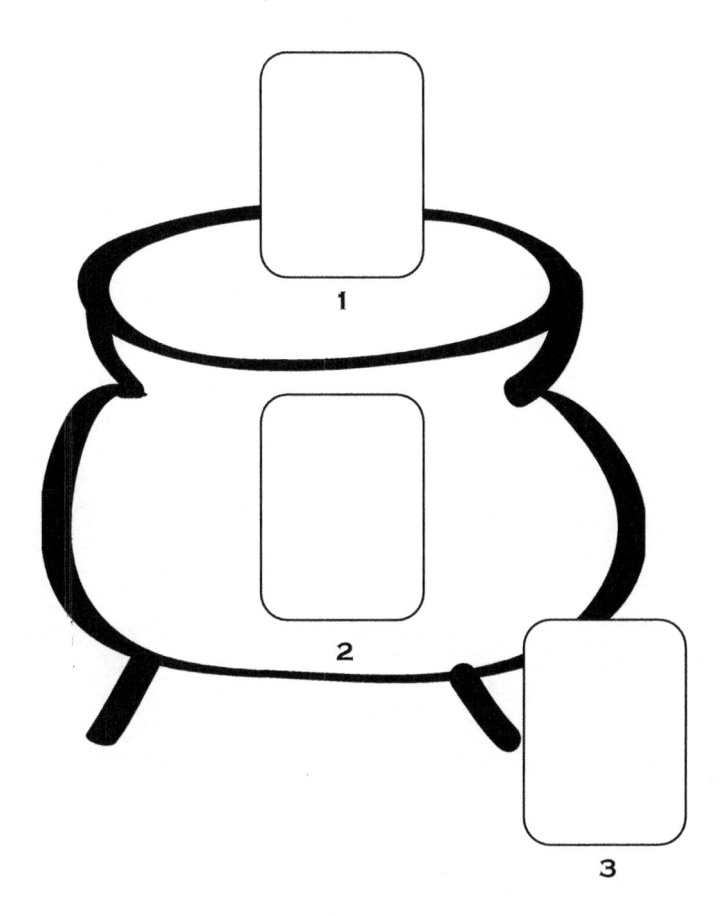

1. What am I bringing to the mix? What am I adding to the Cauldron? What flavors am I mixing in? This might be something I've been reluctant to share or it might be a promise I'm keeping to myself.

2. What needs time to steep to reach its full potential and maximum flavor? What is marinating and soaking and reaching for deepness and richness and complexity? What does my body need? What does she know?

3. What am I serving up? What am I offering? When it is time for the feast, what will I share?

Three Cauldrons

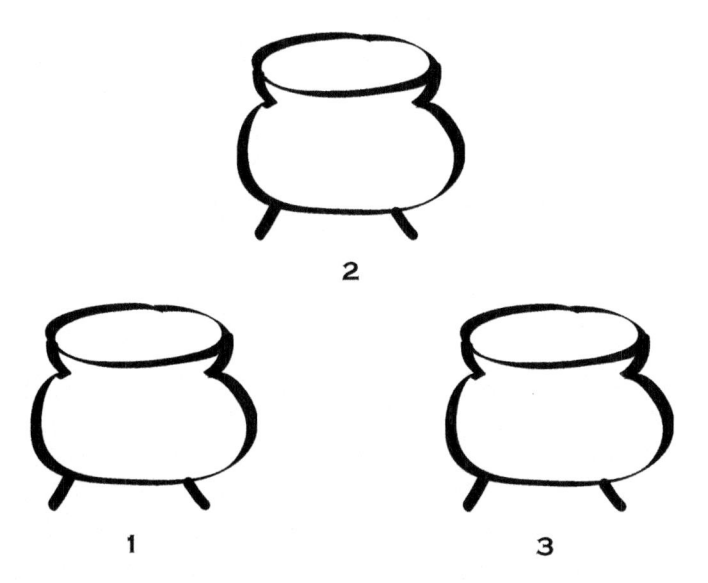

1. **Vitality:** How is my physical body feeling? How are my body and mind working together? Do I feel unified and enlivened? Strong and focused? Choose a card as a reminder, encouragement, inspiration, or affirmation of what is needed to keep this cauldron tended.

2. **Connection:** How are my relationships? Am I feeling connected to myself, friends, partners, family, and community? How do we inspire one another? Do I feel as if I have somewhere I belong and am I attached to others? Choose a card as a reminder, encouragement, inspiration, or affirmation of what is needed to keep this cauldron tended.

3. **Contribution:** How do I feel about my work in the world, whether paid or otherwise? What are my strengths, creative gifts, visions? Where do I find deep meaning? What lights me up with purpose and passion? Choose a card as a reminder, encouragement, inspiration, or affirmation of what is needed to keep this cauldron tended.

Cave Time Layout
(The Dark Moon)

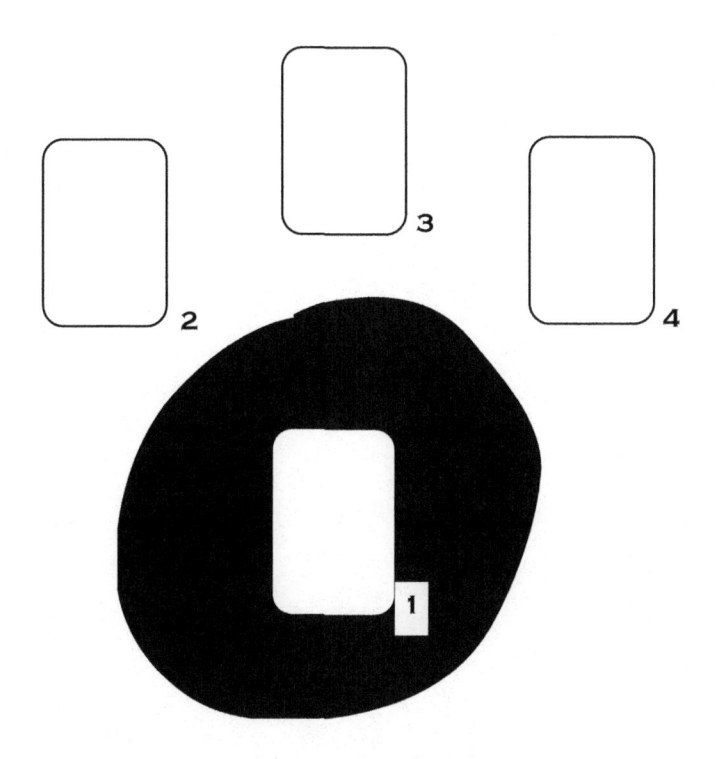

1. **Signifier card**: me (in my cave of darkness)

2. **Contemplation card**: reflection, evaluation, what's on my mind, how are my thoughts affecting me?

3. **Action card**: what am I celebrating, how am I moving forward, what's next?

4. **Realization card**: what is coming into the light, being reborn or renewed? What is emerging after my time in the cave?

The Flying Woman

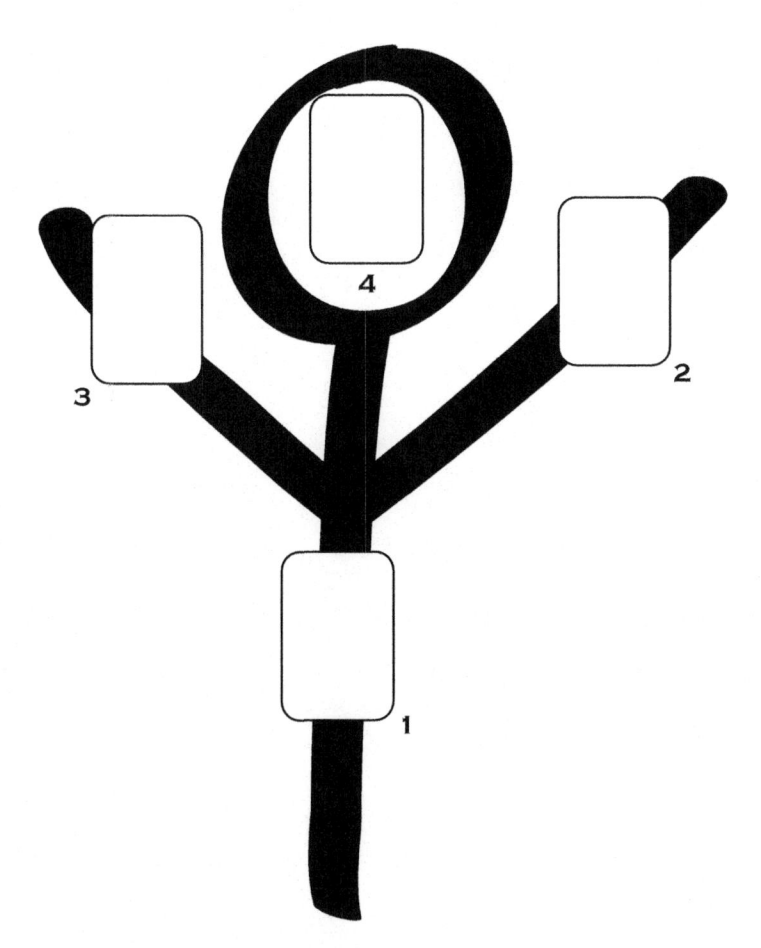

1. **Unearthing:** What has been waiting below the surface? How am I digging deep?

2. **Becoming:** What does the Flying Woman want for me?

3. **Letting go:** Open your fingers and release… Take a deep breath. How do you feel in your center as you let go?

4. **Spinning:** Where is freedom found for me? What is dancing before me?

The Flame

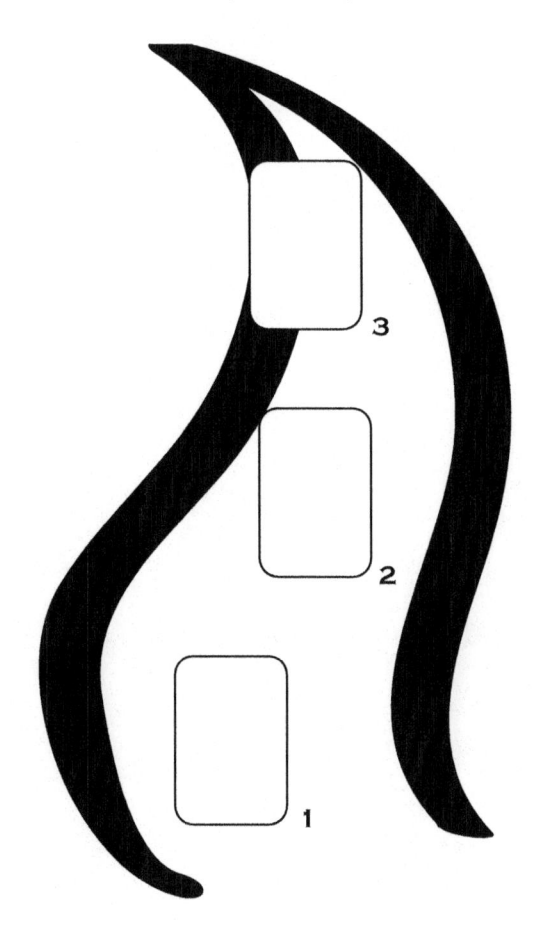

1. **Kindling:** What needs my attention now? How am I feeding my flame, my passion, my energy?

2. **Igniting:** What lights me up? What helps me grow? How do I access my inner warrior?

3. **Tending:** What do I need to grow in my power, to tend my inner fire, to fan the flames of my passions and purposes?

The Tree

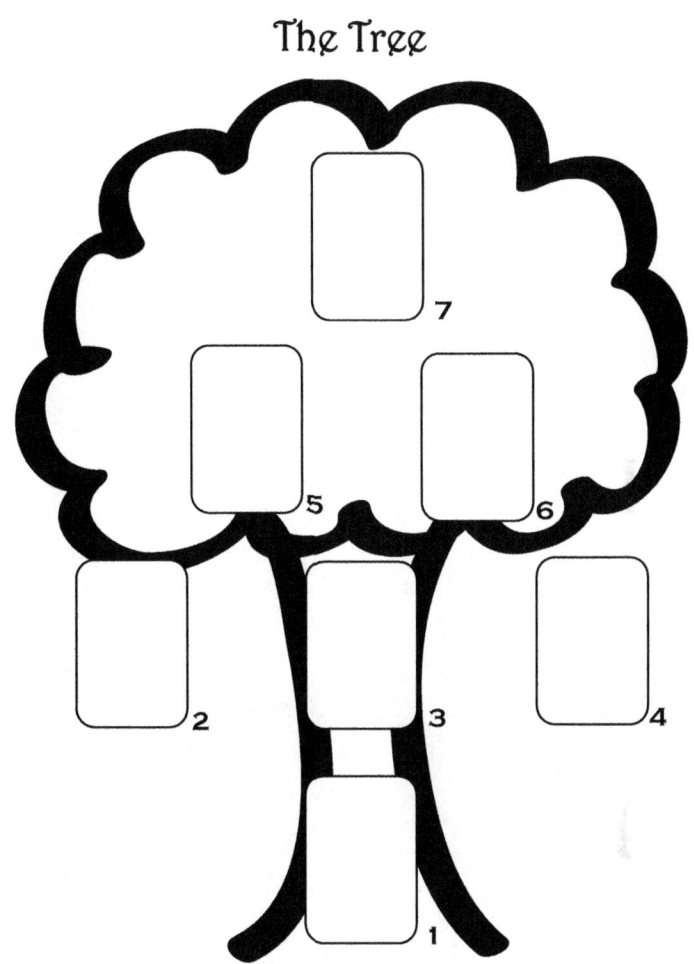

1. My ideas/inspiration
2. What is growing for me
3. What I give
4. My plans
5. Process for bringing plans into being
6. Be attentive to… [potential obstacle]
7. My gift—what emerges (resolution/completion)

The Sun

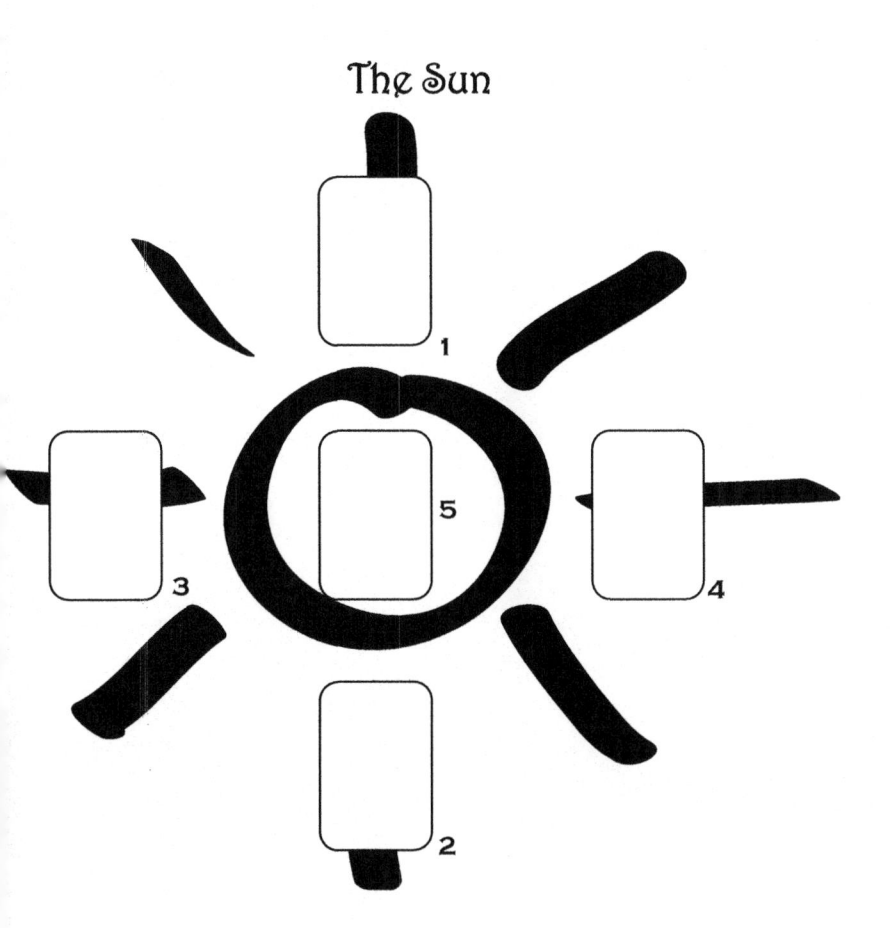

1. Healing needed
2. Healing available
3. Trying again...
4. Creating and offering...
5. Core resource

-OR-

1. Bringing into the light...
2. Still in need of nurturing within dark and quiet spaces
3. What is blooming for me?
4. What is withering in the heat?
5. Time to celebrate...

The Sun & Moon

1. Trust myself...
2. Let it go and laugh...
3. I am free...

-OR-

1. Where do I need to smile and laugh?
2. What/where do I need to let go and shake off?
3. What freedom am I seeking/desiring?

The Cauldron of Reflection

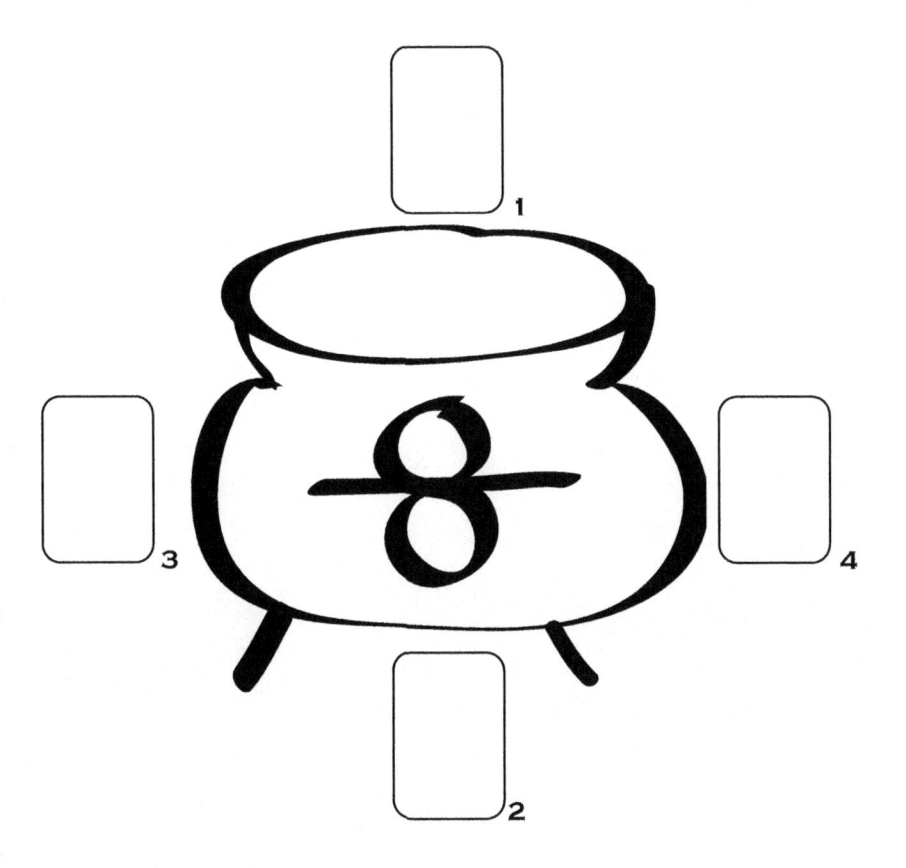

1. What is being created?
2. What is crying out to be heard?
3. What am I steeping?
4. Support card/guiding message.

Claim Your Magic
(Witch's Hat Layout)

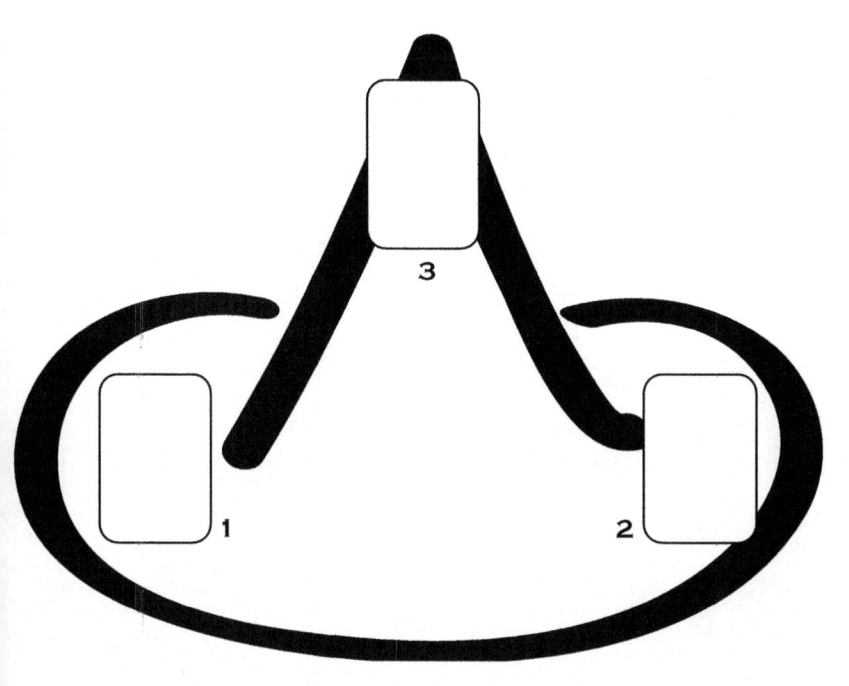

1. What am I afraid of?
2. What is my magic?
3. Action. How to get there?

The Egg

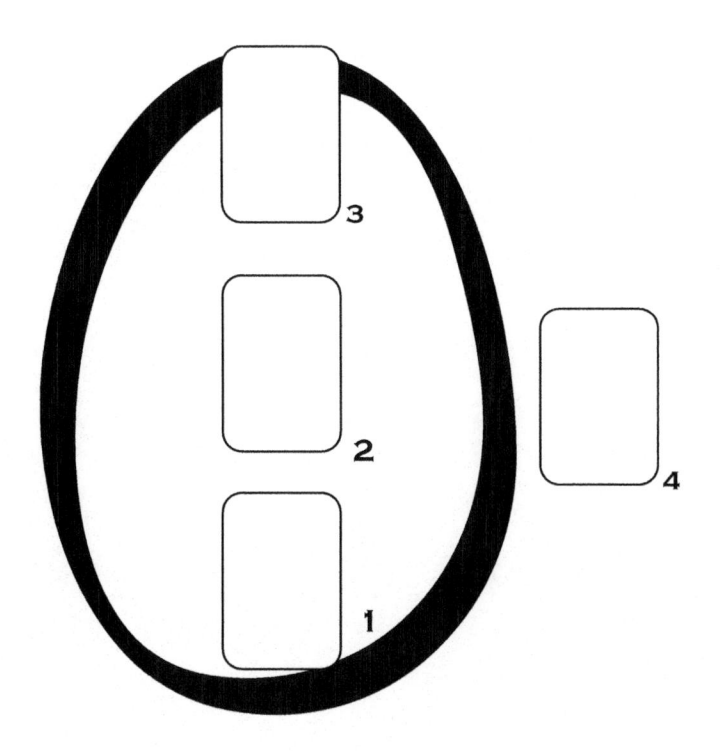

1. What am I naming? (and claiming)
2. Where do I need to clarify my communications? (or need clarity in communication *or* need to communicate about)
3. Listen to this...
4. The answer...I am heard in this way...

The Pentacle (Elemental Layout)

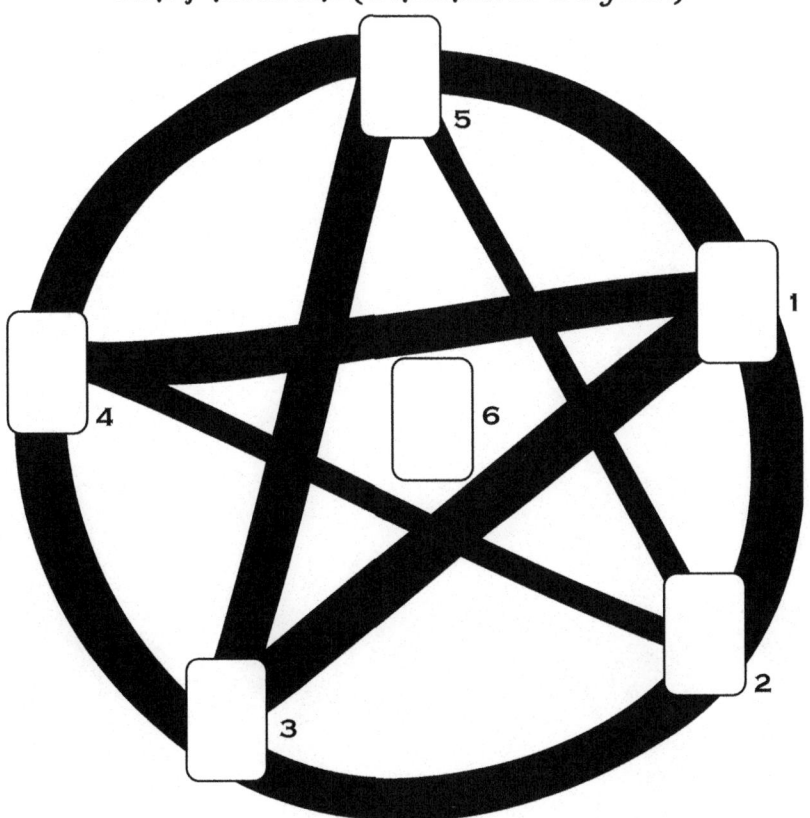

1. Earth: What does my body need? What will ground and center me?

2. Air: Where does my mental focus need to be?

3. Fire: What do I need to know about my broader purpose? How am I feeding my spirit? What do I need to move forward?

4. Water: How do I want to feel? What feeling might I need to express/experience? (or, release!)

5. Spirit: Divine guidance/ goddess wisdom/message from source or guides.

6. Card of the month/guiding card (and/or use this space to create a bindrune with your other five runes)

The Dancing Woman

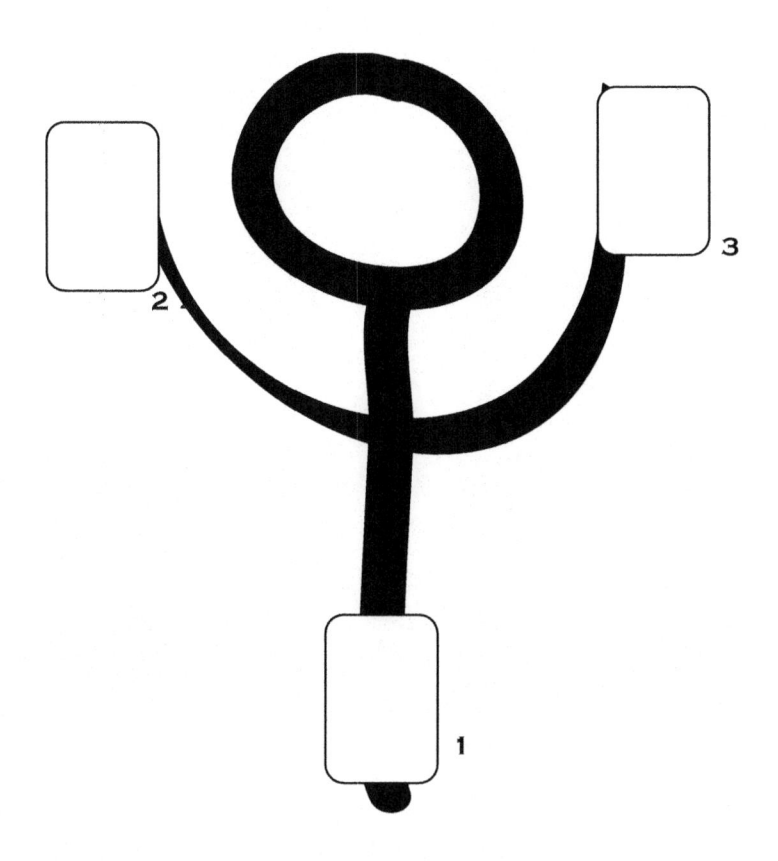

1. Base of power (what am I dancing on or with?)

2. The power moving through me, my inherent power source.

3. What is longing to be expressed?

The Two Triangles

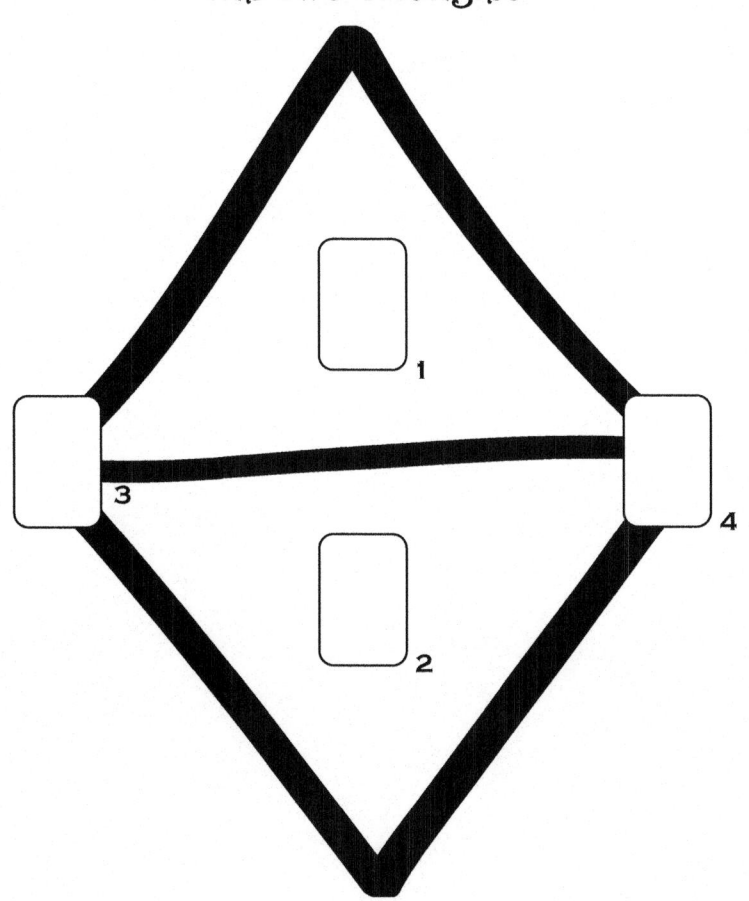

1. Focus on...

2. An area of choice (note: you may also wish to position this card in reverse and consider its potential "opposite" meaning).

3. What is still fuzzy/needs support/clarity?

4. Support card/guiding rune.

Engaging with the Runes

How to make your own Womanrunes

There are many ways to make your own set of Womanrunes. I suggest making several different kinds of sets to serve different purposes or settings. A basic means is to etch each symbol on a disk of polymer clay, self-hardening clay, oven-hardening clay, or pottery clay (later fired in a kiln).

An even simpler method is to use permanent markers to draw each Womanrune on a pebble, a beach rock, a seashell, or a wooden circle or other shape.

Another simple method is to draw each symbol on card stock or small index cards. Write the name of each rune beneath the symbol for easy reference for divination.

You may use glass paint markers to draw each rune on a glass pebbles from a craft store or pet store (often sold as material for aquariums). The paint is then fired in your kitchen oven and becomes resistant to scratching.

Using permanent markers to draw each rune on small squares of fabric is another easy possibility. You might also choose to embroider the Womanrunes on fabric squares.

Cosmic Wink Cards

"The word 'rune' originates in words meaning 'secret,' but 'rune' has also come to mean 'a poem, charm, or spell.' Runar (from the Norse) means 'a magical sign,' and runa (from Old German) is 'to whisper a secret.' 'Hidden,' 'magic,' 'whispers,' all words long associated with Faery, the secret country. So when we talk of runes, we are speaking of objects that have multiple meanings, letters both worldly and otherworldly in origin and aspect. Their 'secrets' may not reside so much in hidden meanings, but in ways of seeing the world. In this sense, each single rune creates layers of phonetics, poetry, and power built up over time. Runes are intended to endure. They record things that must be remembered or heeded. Runes are letters and words that must not be lost or wasted. They embody and express essential knowledge..."
–Brian Froud, *Runes of Elfland*

Several years ago I had laryngitis and was completely mute. I woke up in the morning with a crystal clear vision of the earth, suspended in space, feeling awe-struck at the majesty and complexity of this planet whirling through space, part of the vast, unfathomable universe. It seemed so clear to me that I was seeing the "invisible net of incarnation" of which we are all a part, the earth held in this enormous web of the universe. Upon rising for the day, I was thinking about my ideas about divinity and reflecting on my cosmological view of the universe as the body of the Goddess and the idea that the very web of life itself *is* the Goddess. Accompanying the sense of majesty was then a profound sense of *impersonality*. How can I possibly connect personally with something so vast and so powerful? So, as I sat that morning at my little corner altar in the living room, I asked (silently—I had laryngitis, remember!): "what do I need to know about the *personalization* of the divine?" I drew a *Crone Stone* from my little bag by the altar...

Remember the laryngitis and then also imagine the huge smile on my face when the stone I drew was, The Speaker, with the questions included in the interpretation, "is your voice being heard?" and "how will you share your voice with the world?" And then the final message, **"let your voice pour forth like a flowing river..."** At this moment I felt I had received an answer to my wonderings—that the Goddess is *both* as enormous and impersonal as my vision of the web holding the earth and yet also personal enough to offer me this cosmic wink through my Crone Stone.

As I completed the first edition of this book, the final symbol I wrote about was The Sun and Moon, the rune of laughter. *"Are you afraid to laugh?"* the rune asked me and I had to confront how little time I afford myself for fun and amusement as I keep up with the demands of the day. This rune became a touchstone for me and we used it on the front cover of the book as a reminder to keep enjoyment in our work. As I continued to work with the runes, I began to realize that the Sun and Moon is my "cosmic wink" Womanrunes card. It turns up whenever I need a nudge, a reminder, a boost of encouragement, a reminder that I'm on the right track. It never fails to make me smile and I can *feel* it coming. As I work with other people and Womanrunes, I notice that many of them receive a cosmic wink card of their own. It might be one that feels frustrating to see emerge, *again*. Or, it might be one that speaks to a private joke (such as my laryngitis experience). It might be one that feels initially confusing, but whose meaning and relevance becomes clear with time. It might be one that turns up at exactly the right moment. You will come to know and recognize, celebrate and love, your cosmic wink card. It is an affirmation that the divinity is personal and that you're not alone.

People also often notice that Womanrunes have a distinct sense of humor. They like to play little jokes and they're "cheeky," as many women have told me. For example, when I wrote about The Veil, the rune of mystery and that which is unknown, it slipped out of my hand and fell through the cracks in the porch, thus literally becoming veiled and unseen by me.

How to identify your own cosmic wink card (in any system):
- Is there a card that shows up for you routinely, more than the others?

- Is there a card that often jumps or falls from the deck?
- Is there a card that sometimes feels like a "chastisement" or almost a rebuke? ("not *this* again?!")
- Is there a card that makes you laugh as soon as you see it—like, *message received.*
- Is there a card that you are often able to *feel* coming?
- Is there a rune that shows up in your dreams or guided meditations or that you find yourself doodling or thinking about?

In Womanrunes, sometimes your cosmic wink card will also magically show up as part of the spelling of your own name.

"...Whatever the Runes may be—a bridge between the self and Self, a link between the Self and the Divine, an ageless navigational aid—the energy that engages them is our own, and, ultimately, the wisdom as well. Thus, as we start to make contact with our Knowing Selves, we will begin to hear messages of profound beauty and true usefulness. For like snowflakes and fingerprints, each of our oracular signatures is a one-of-a-kind aspect of Creation addressing its own."

–Ralph Blum, The Book of Runes, p. 34-35

Womanrunes with Groups

There are lots of special ways to bring the womanspirit wisdom of Womanrunes in your Women's Circle, Red Tent, retreats, or rituals. Here are some possibilities:

- Have the Womanrunes deck and book available in a divination or intuition corner. This nook should be a reflective space for inner guidance.
- Lay out the cards and book on a table close to the entrance of the ritual space. As women enter, they can draw a card to receive a personal check-in with their deep selves.
- As the circle begins, the cards may be passed around the circle as a basic guidance or intuition check or as a centering process. Women may share their reflections or observations or journal about the message.
- Likewise, Womanrunes may be used to check-out once the circle is drawing to a close. Before singing your final song or doing your closing reading, each woman can draw a card and read the interpretation as her message or guidance for her return home.
- If you include meditations, guided visualizations, or discussion prompts in your circle, Womanrunes may be used before or after journaling about these experiences.

Using Womanrunes on Group Projects

- Make prayer flags—either drawing on the symbols using permanent markers or stitching or embroidering them on. You can sew a small channel across the top of each flag and then insert a dowel rode into them to make a rotating system of prayer flag rune messages.
- Make single flags with certain runes (either intentionally chosen or intuitively chosen).
- Make personal sets of Womanrunes for use at home using any of the methods described in this book.
- Make goddess greeting cards with written greetings, blessings, or wishes
- Create runespells by combining symbols for personal messages.
- Write your name or a word of power using the pronunciation guide handout.
- Create a pocket touchstone or a reminder stone with polymer clay or pottery clay. On this touchstone, you can include the Womanrunes you'd like to attract, manifest, or embody. Or, you can write your name or other word. You may also intuitively select which symbols to include.
- Paint Womanrunes on yourself or in group with other women using body paint—this can be done for empowerment, affirmation, encouragement, healing, blessing, or fun.

Deepening into the Runes

*Once she opened
her eyes
she discovered
magic
in all the everyday
corners of the world.*

As you continue with your practice with Womanrunes, becoming confident and comfortable with speaking the language of these runes, here are some additional ideas for deepening into your relationship with, and practical use of, these potently powerful and magical symbols:
- While sitting with your rune of the day in a safe place and perhaps with music playing, drape a scarf or cloth over your head and silently *feel into* the rune. What does it have to tell you today?
- After your daily rune, pay attention to signs from nature, from Gaia. What does her rhythm have to tell you today?
- Notice your dreams. How do they change as you work with the runes?
- Make art with the symbols themselves: carve them on a candle or into clay for a pocket touchstone. Try simply doodling the rune of the day. No pressure or other expectation. Just doodle it and then doodle other images or words around it.
- Rewrite a quote or keywords from this book into

your own handwriting. Be creative with how you re-write it and experiment with making different words different sizes, colors, and so on.
- Turn the rune card of the day over in the deck so it is facing out in the clear lid of the card box. Then, keep it near you during the day. It isn't necessary to wait for perfect timing or perfect space, let it come with you where and when you are.
- It is okay for the day's experience to be "small." It may even be unnoticeable at first until you tune in, and as Mary Oliver said, "pay attention and be astonished."
- Keep your eyes open for synchronicities. Womanrunes speak to something deep within us and if you are alert, you will see them at work in your world and life, sometimes very subtly.
- Look for lessons in unexpected places and from unexpected sources.

Live this. Don't wait for a perfect time. Carry yourself through the day in awareness and notice the message when it comes. It might be in an unexpected place. You may have to stretch, reach, and dig to find it. Sometimes all I can do in a day is carry the card with me to the woods and take a picture of it. That's okay too.

Wait for the magic. Notice the magic. Be surprised. Be open.

Stretching into a Rune...

When I suggest stretching into a rune, I mean making a connection to a rune that doesn't seem to initially speak to you. For me, the stretching comes in being alert to subtleties rather than big flashes. I will use The Two Triangles as an example, but you can insert any of the cards into this stretching process, which is particularly helpful if you're having trouble connecting with a specific rune.

To stretch, I keep the card turned over right near I am working (and inked on my wrist using liquid eyeliner) and whenever I glance at it, I let the themes of that rune come to mind: *clean edges* (or whatever it is for the day). Hmm. Then my attention goes back to whatever I'm doing. I spot the rune again. It is like a mindfulness trigger. Clean edges. Where are they showing up today? What am I *not* noticing? I read the words on the card and let them swim around for a while. Focus. Analysis. Rationality. I go back to the work, but in the background the words are there. Focus. Analysis. Clean edges. I notice that what I am actually doing *at this moment* is analyzing student papers. Hmm. The Two Triangles rune *is* showing up, it just isn't fun. I remember that I *have* to be focused to finish grading. I have to let go of other plans for today and just buckle down and *focus*. I take my computer over to the printer and set it on the counter. I notice the clean edges of my laptop. How it contains all this analytical, focused work. I notice, I kid you not, the straight-edge ruler completely coincidentally sitting on the counter right behind my laptop. Clean edges. Right there. **The Two Triangles.**

The *stretching* for me is in not letting it go and thinking, "this one isn't working," it is continuing to pay attention, let the words swirl and marinate and then, ah ha! *There it is.* Being open to the appearance even when it isn't fun, flashy, or even very interesting!

Runewriting

One of Shekhinah's purposes in creating the Womanrunes was to create a woman-identified alphabet writing system. On the original pronunciation guide included in this book (p. 201), you will find the correspondences between each Womanrune and the English language. You may use runewriting to write your own name or to write messages on cards to your friends. I've used runewriting with my family to create pocket touchstones for power, courage, and inspiration as well.

Sample

Rune

Writing

Bindrunes

A bindrune is a new rune created purposefully through the combination of several runes. These runes are bound together or combined to give additional meanings or symbols. You can create a bindrune of your own name or other word or concept.

The name Brigid in runewriting

Runewritten name combined into a bindrune.

Runespells

Combining related Womanrunes into bindrunes can also create a runespell. For example:

Will **Power** **Willpower**

"Runespells can be done in a number of ways. A single rune can be used as an affirmation to bring desired results. The Love Rune, for example, can be used to bring or strengthen love. Draw it on a piece of paper and place it in a magical pouch on your altar. Etch or paint it on a special stone; rose quartz for example..." (Womanrunes booklet, p. 17).

You may also make runesigns over things you wish to bless or infuse with runic meaning or power.

Pocket Touchstone

Create a round disk. Onto the surface of the disk, etch your name in Womanrunes as well as other runes that you wish to attract, remember, or learn from. Fire or bake the clay and then carry the touchstone close to you as a reminder of your own power, potential, and purpose.

Inking Womanrunes

A very simple yet powerful practice with Womanrunes is to draw them onto your body. I learned from one of my students to use liquid eyeliner to ink the symbol of the day (chosen in the morning as a centering or guidance practice or consciously chosen as something you'd like to keep in the forefront of your day) on the inside of the wrist or ankle. This symbol then serves as a mindfulness or guidance cue throughout day. The process of inking the symbols on your skin is a beautifully embodied, physical practice that makes a visceral connection to Womanrunes. You are literally *drawing them into you.*

This inking of the runes is a simple, powerful, quick, connected practice. The physical connection is powerful and you can even create runespells on your body. It feels like a little secret to carry through the day *and* if it is right there on your wrist, you will have many occasions to see it throughout the day where it serves as little mindfulness bell as well as a reminder to *pay attention.*

In PMH Atwater's book, *Runes of the Goddess*, she explains:

Indeed, long before there was ever a need for hieroglyphic script, there must have been a desire and a passion for recreating patterns in the mind that would evoke the immediacy of special moments. These special moments would have been no less than ones where earth and sky, heaven and human, seemed to merge, intermingling the invisible with the visible. Such would have been times of awe and wonder... when spirit reigned.

These patterns in the mind would have quickly become anchored in collective memory because of their connection to basic comprehension levels and survival urges...

These patterns in the mind are the real runes.

(Atwater, p. 135)

May these Womanrunes help you understand the richness of your own mind, the depth of your own intuition, and the power and potentiality of the vast Womanspirit that enfolds us all.

WOMANRUNES

0. The Circle, Rune of Self
1. The Witches' Hat, Rune of Magic
2. The Crescent Moon, Rune of Divination
3. The Yoni, Rune of Making
4. The Flame, Rune of Fire
5. The Heart, Rune of Love
6. The Labyris, Rune of Will
7. The Dancing Woman, Rune of Power
8. The Box, Rune of Limitation
9. The Dark Moon, Rune of Wisdom
10. The Wheel, Rune of Fate
11. The Pendulum, Rune of Karma
12. The Reflection, Rune of Surrender
13. The Flying Woman, Rune of Transformation
14. The Cauldron, Rune of Alchemy
15. The Whole Moon, Rune of Psyche
16. The Serpent, Rune of Awakening
17. The Moon & Star, Rune of Faith
18. The Sun, Rune of Healing
19. The Dancing Women, Rune of Celebration
20. The Great Wheel, Rune of Infinity
21. The Egg, Rune of Naming
22. The Sisters, Rune of Friendship
23. The Seed, Rune of Waiting
24. The Tool, Rune of Labor
25. The Winged Circle, Rune of Freedom
26. The Cauldron of Reflection, Rune of Solitude
27. The Crowned Heart, Rune of Compassion
28. The Tree, Rune of Prosperity
29. The Pentacle, Rune of Protection
30. The Two Circles, Rune of Merging
31. The Two Triangles, Rune of Focus
32. The Moonboat, Rune of Journeys
33. The Hearth, Rune of Nurturance
34. The Cauldron of Dancing Women, Rune of Honor
35. The Broom, Rune of Purification
36. The Spiral, Rune of Initiation
37. The Wand, Rune of Blessing
38. The Sun & Moon, Rune of Laughter
39. The Winged Heart, Rune of Ecstasy
40. The Veil, Rune of Mystery...

Please keep system intact - Thanks!

© 1988 Shekhinah Mountainwater
New Edition Jan. 2, 001
Please use and acknowledge

O – with voice
Ø – without voice

WOMANRUNES ©
Pronunciation Guide

0. "I" as in h<u>i</u>gh
1. "W" as in <u>w</u>itch
2. "L" as in <u>l</u>ove
3. "M" as in <u>m</u>other
4. "R" as in roa<u>r</u>
5. "AH" as in m<u>a</u>ma
6. "B" as in <u>b</u>ig / "P" as in <u>p</u>ush
7. "oo" as in b<u>oo</u>k
8. "ng" as in wi<u>ng</u>
9. "J" as in <u>j</u>ay / "ch" as in <u>ch</u>ild
10. "ĭ" as in <u>i</u>t
11. "ă" as in <u>a</u>t
12. "ŭ" as in <u>u</u>p (the bending vowel)
13. "N" as in <u>n</u>ow
14. "ĕ" as in w<u>e</u>t
15. "ee" as in s<u>ee</u>
16. "ss" as in <u>s</u>assy / "zz" as in <u>z</u>oo
17. "oo" as in s<u>oo</u>n
18. "aw" as in s<u>aw</u>
19. "Y" as in <u>y</u>es
20. "ō" as in sl<u>o</u>w
21. "h" as in <u>h</u>ome
22. "K" as in <u>k</u>iss / "G" as in <u>g</u>ood
23. "sh" as in <u>sh</u>e / "zh" as in vi<u>s</u>ion
24. "F" as in <u>f</u>ine / "V" as in <u>v</u>ote
25. "Th" as in <u>th</u>ick / "th" as in <u>th</u>en
26. "ea" as in b<u>ea</u>r
27. "au" as in n<u>ow</u>
28. "T" as in <u>t</u>ipi / "D" as in <u>d</u>og
29. "Ā" as in st<u>ay</u>
30. African click
31. Welsh/German/Hebrew guttural "chh"
32. French "R"
33. French nasal as in "sans"
34. "ě" as in h<u>e</u>r
35. Rolled "R" rrrrr
36. "wh" as in <u>wh</u>ere
37. "ua" as in K<u>o</u>re
38. Gasping - the indrawn breath
39. "oi" as in <u>oy</u> vay
     Silence

PLEASE KEEP SYSTEM INTACT

©1988 Shekhinah Mountainwater
New edition Jan. 2001
Please use and acknowledge

Shakti Woman Speaks

Shakti woman speaks.
She says Dance
Write
Create
Share
Speak.
Don't let me down.
I wait within
coiled at the base of your spine,
draped around your hips
like a bellydancer's sash,
snaking my way up
through your belly
and your throat
until I burst forth
in radiant power
that shall not be denied.
Do not silence me.
Do not coil my energy back inside
stuffing it down
where it might wither in darkness
biding its time
becoming something that waits
to strike.
Let me sing.
Let me flood through your body
in ripples of ecstasy.
Stretch your hands wide,
wear jewels on your fingers
and your heart on your sleeve.
Spin.
Spin with me now
until we dance shadows into art
hope into being
and pain into power.

About the Author

Molly is a priestess, writer, teacher, and artist who lives with her husband and children in Missouri. She holds master's degrees in both clinical social work and in goddess studies and a doctorate of ministry degree in goddess spirituality. Molly and her husband Mark co-create Story Goddesses and other original goddess art, mini goddesses, ceremony kits, and goddess grids at Brigid's Grove: brigidsgrove.etsy.com and she blogs about thealogy, nature, practical priestessing, and the goddess at brigidsgrove.com.

Acknowledgments

Shekhinah Mountainwater for the very idea, the symbols, and the beginnings.

Joy Harjo in the anthology *Open Mind* for the phrase "night wind woman" (used in opening poem).

Anne Key for the image of the heart kneaded by Sekhmet's claws (in *Desert Priestess: A Memoir*).

Wayne Dyer for the concept of "playing your music" and for the reminder, "don't argue with reality."

Bayard Rustin for the phrase "speak truth to power."

Mary Oliver for the words "pay attention and be astonished."

Martin Luther King, Jr. for the phrase "arc of the universe."

Andrea Potos for the phrase "unclench your life."

Syren Nagakyrie for the contact and for the idea of inking the runes.

SageWoman Magazine (www.sagewoman.com) for sparking my curiosity about Womanrunes more than

24 years after actually publishing the article!

Global Goddess (www.globalgoddess.org) email list for additional information about Womanrunes and for helping me excavate old information from the depths of the internet.

Karen Orozco for author photograph, p. 203.

Amy Terrill, Barbara Johnson, Phanie Stuckey, Jenny Johnson, and Shellei Kittrell for *showing up*.

Mark Remer for love, for always being a soft place to land, for co-creation, for co-parenting, and for looking outward in the same direction.

Barbara and Tom Johnson for trust, faith, confidence, love, and childcare.

Resources

Ariadne's Thread by Shekhinah Mountainwater available used from online booksellers (plus her little booklet *Womanrunes*, sometimes available from: shekhinah.net)

Crone Stones by Carol Lee Campbell. Available from cronestones.com. I absolutely *love* this set and the book that goes with it. Extremely powerful.

The Gaian Tarot by Joanna Colbert. My very favorite tarot deck. Earth-honoring, insightful, beautiful, and practical. gaiantarot.com

The Goddess Speaks oracle deck and accompanying book by Dee Poth (available from used booksellers).

Listening to the Oracle by Dianne Skafte. An excellent book about cultivating "oracular space" and listening to the ensouled world.

Runes of the Goddess by PMH Atwater (pmhatwater.hypermart.net).

Free Introduction to Womanrunes Class

brigidsgrove.com/womanrunes

Come Join the Circle!

Membership in the Creative Spirit Circle is FREE and packed with beautiful, bountiful resources, including:

- a free Womanrunes e-course
- Companion online classroom
- Goddess Studies and Ritual course
- weekly virtual circles in our Facebook group
- Red Tent, sacred ceremony, and ritual resources
- goddess mandalas and worksheets
- access to Divine Imperfections sculptures
- monthly *Creative Spirit Circle Journal* filled with resources such as ceremony outlines, articles, book recommendations, sneak peeks, and special freebies.

Claim your place in the Circle:
brigidsgrove.com/come-join-the-circle

Connect with Brigid's Grove

- brigidsgrove.com
- facebook.com/brigidsgrove
- instagram.com/brigidsgrove
- brigidsgrove.etsy.com
- Creative Spirit Circle Facebook Group: facebook.com/groups/brigidsgrovecreativespiritcircle

Printed in Great Britain
by Amazon